THE SMUDGING AND BLESSINGS BOOK

THE SMUDGING AND BLESSINGS BOOK

Inspirational rituals to cleanse and heal

JANE ALEXANDER

A GODSFIELD BOOK

Library of Congress Cataloging-in-Publication Data Available

10 9 8 7 6 5 4 3 2 1

Published in 1999 by Sterling Publishing Company, Inc.
387 Park Avenue South, New York, N.Y. 10016

DESIGNED FOR GODSFIELD PRESS BY
THE BRIDGEWATER BOOK COMPANY LTD

Picture Research *Lynda Marshall*
Illustrations *Kim Glass*
Studio Photography *Walter Gardiner Photographers*

Distributed in Canada by Sterling Publishing
c/o Canadian Manda Group, One Atlantic Avenue, Suite 105
Toronto, Ontario, Canada M6K 3E7
Distributed in Australia by Capricorn Link (Australia) Pty Ltd
P O. Box 6651, Baulkham Hills, Business Centre, NSW 2153, Australia

Manufactured in China

Sterling ISBN 0-8069-3149-3

The publishers would like to thank the following for the use of pictures:
The Bridgeman Art Library: pp. 9t, 11, 25t, 34/35, 41, 64, 76
e.t.archive: pp. 70, 80, 92
Fortean Picture Library: p. 74
The Garden Picture Library: p. 72
Hutchison Library: p. 8
The Image Bank: pp. 9b, 10t, 10b, 22, 40, 49, 51t, 55, 56, 58, 62, 65, 68, 69, 70/71, 73, 81, 82l, 86b, 86t, 90
The Stock Market: pp. 18, 25, 46, 59, 61, 75t, 83, 94
Werner Forman Archive: pp. 19, 20, 32l, 50, 53t, 87, 89, 95

CONTENTS

INTRODUCTION

SMUDGING IS THE COMMON NAME GIVEN TO THE SACRED SMOKE BOWL BLESSING, A POWERFUL CLEANSING TECHNIQUE FROM THE NATIVE NORTH AMERICAN TRADITION. SMUDGING CALLS ON THE SPIRITS OF SACRED PLANTS TO DRIVE AWAY NEGATIVE ENERGIES AND RESTORE BALANCE. IT IS THE ART OF CLEANSING YOURSELF AND YOUR ENVIRONMENT USING SIMPLE RITUAL AND CEREMONY. FOR THOUSANDS OF YEARS SMUDGING HAS BEEN A PART OF NATIVE AMERICAN TRADITION BUT NOW ITS POWER OF CLEANSING IS AVAILABLE TO EVERYONE.

Native North Americans in traditional costume. Their rituals have been a source of inspiration across the world.

THE POWER OF SMUDGING

How can smudging be so powerful? The answer lies in the subatomic world of subtle or spiritual energy. Homes and bodies are not just made of purely physical matter; they also vibrate with quiet, invisible energy. Cleansing a space or our bodies with techniques such as smudging clears away all the emotional and psychic "garbage" that may have gathered over years or even hundreds of years. It's like spiritual spring cleaning.

The effects of smudging can be surprisingly swift and dramatic. The rituals in this book can help you banish stress and attract love, soothe you, or give you energy. They can bring your family closer together and let you adjust to the healing seasonal rhythms of the year. Above all, they can turn any space, however humble, into a soothing sanctuary – a place of renewal and happiness. In this book we combine smudging with techniques from other ancient traditions to provide a totally holistic approach.

AN AGE-OLD TRADITION

Many Western churches burn incense during their religious ceremonies in order to cleanse a sacred space.

These ideas are not newfangled, nor are they airy-fairy new-age waffle. Native North American tradition dates back millennia, and most traditional cultures – from the Zulus to the Maoris, from the Chinese to the Balinese – have age-old forms of cleansing and blessing rituals. Even the West retains relics of them, although we have long forgotten the true purpose behind many such rituals and ceremonies. Incense wafting through a church cleanses the atmosphere just as surely as the medicine man's bowl of sacred smoke, or smudge. The bells that ring out on Sunday are intended to purify the whole parish and lead the community into worship, just as the shaman's drum can lead us on sacred journeys to the spirit world.

This pack will provide you with all the information that you need to start smudging and to perform your own cleansings, rituals, and blessings. Approach this work with a pure heart, an open mind, and a sense of adventure: it could change your entire life...

By smudging and blessing you can learn to find tranquility in union with nature.

THE HISTORY OF SMUDGING

SMUDGING MAY SEEM A VERY MODERN PRACTICE; WE READ ABOUT CITY HIGHFLIERS USING IT TO SELL THEIR APARTMENTS OR IMPROVE THEIR BUSINESS LUCK, BUT SMUDGING HAS BEEN USED FOR THOUSANDS OF YEARS. WHEN YOU LIGHT A SMUDGE STICK YOU ARE CONNECTING WITH A SPIRITUAL TRADITION THAT ORIGINATES FROM THE DEPTHS OF TIME.

The tradition of burning herbs is probably age-old and is internationally accepted.

A TRADITION FROM THE MISTS OF TIME

It is impossible to say for certain when smudging began. Perhaps early civilizations came to realize, through sheer trial and error, that the smoke generated by setting alight particular herbs had beneficial effects for humanity. Certainly many cultures have an old tradition of driving animals through the smoke to kill off pests and diseases. Nowadays modern science has proven that certain herbs do indeed have cleansing powers, acting as

In a similar ritual to smudging, a Buddhist monk meditates to the smell of burning incense.

strong pesticides. Aside from this beneficial and practical aspect of burning herbs, humans have become aware that smoke ascends to the heavens – to the world of spirits – almost as if it were acting as a spiritual messenger.

This painting by John William Waterhouse depicts a priest burning herbs in a Greek temple during a ritual to cure a sick child. It has long been accepted that herbs have healing properties.

The idea of purification through smoke is certainly not the sole preserve of the Native North Americans. Most rituals have some element of cleansing, and incense or herbal smoke mixtures are burned around the world – from China, India, and Southeast Asia to Europe and the Western world.

THE NATIVE AMERICAN WAY

Originally, mixtures of sacred herbs and resins were burned in a special bowl. Smoke was then wafted around the person or place needing purification and cleansing. However, smudge sticks (bundles of dried herbs tied together with colored thread or a strip of hide) offer an easier way of smudging that is just as effective.

The herbs most often used in smudge sticks are sage and sweetgrass. Sage drives out any negative thoughts, energies, spirits, and influences. Sweetgrass is used to attract positive energy after all the negative energies have been banished by sage. Native North Americans see smudging as a way of shifting between various levels of reality – connecting us here in the material, physical world to the subtle realm of spirits.

INTRODUCING THE PACK

YOU HAVE WITHIN YOUR PACK EVERYTHING YOU NEED TO PRACTICE SMUDGING AND TO CARRY OUT A LARGE VARIETY OF CLEANSINGS AND BLESSINGS. SMUDGE STICKS, CANDLES, CRYSTALS, AND OILS HAVE BEEN USED FOR CLEANSING AND BLESSING SPACES AND PEOPLE FOR MILLENNIA – NOW YOU TOO CAN UTILIZE THEIR PROTECTIVE POWERS.

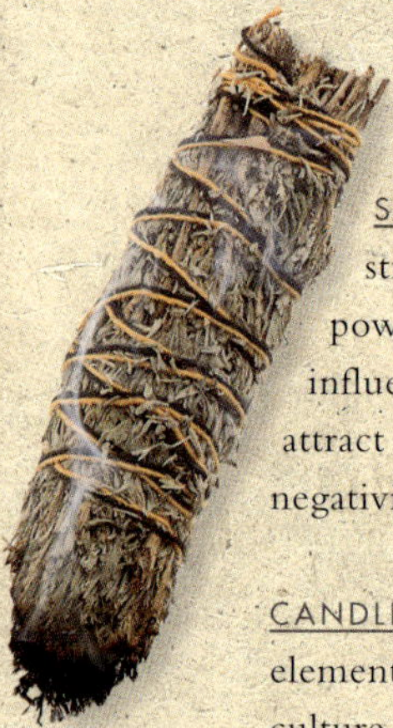

THE CONTENTS OF YOUR KIT

SMUDGE STICK: The herbs most often used in smudge sticks are sage and sweetgrass. The spirit of sage has the power to drive out negative energies, spirits, and influences. The powerful spirit of sweetgrass is used to attract positive energy, and to aid healing after all the negativity has been banished by sage.

CANDLES: A lighted candle represents the element of fire. In Native North American culture fire is considered sacred to the gods. As well as having a purifying effect, it is inspiring and can usher in times of transformation and new ways of living. Fire brings light, courage, and purity of intent.

You can buy a variety of smudge sticks, but the most common include the herb sage.

CRYSTALS: Crystals symbolize the strength and healing of the earth. A crystal will take up your intent and maintain it long after the ritual has been completed. The crystal in this pack is rose quartz. It promotes

The rose quartz crystal, included in this pack, will promote peace.

love and peace, aids self-esteem and creates harmony - both physical and spiritual. You will need to cleanse your crystal before using it – simply immerse it in a bowl of water to which you have added three tablespoons of sea salt. Leave for 72 hours, then take it out and dry it. A clean crystal will be more effective.

This Native North American rattle is made from a tortoise shell, animal skins, and a feather. Drums or rattles can be used to enhance the smudging ceremony.

ADD YOUR OWN OIL

Aromatherapy oils have the ability to affect both our physical bodies and our emotions. They can even influence our spirit. Lavender has traditionally been used to restore balance and create a peaceful atmosphere in the home. It is profoundly calming and soothing, and is said to draw in loving energy.

OTHER USEFUL TOOLS

Although you can perform a huge variety of blessings and cleansings with just these tools, there are a few other items that might prove useful. Some are required for particular rituals in this book. Others you just might like to add to your ceremonies to personalize them, making them your very own.

A small ceramic or **stone bowl** – or **a large shell** – on which to place your smudge stick. Put a little sand in the bottom so that you can safely extinguish the stick after use.

A large feather to waft the smudge.

An oil burner for your aromatherapy oils or a **bowl** in which you can put hot water to float the oils.

Flower essences – such as the Bach, Australian Bush, or FES – that can easily be incorporated into rituals.

Bells, drums, and **rattles,** which, when played, shift energy in a room.

Sea salt to act as a natural purifier.

THE CHAKRAS

ACCORDING TO EASTERN PHILOSOPHY, OUR BODIES CONTAIN SEVEN MAJOR ENERGY CENTERS, KNOWN AS THE CHAKRAS. THEY CAN BE VISUALIZED AS SPINNING WHEELS OF ENERGY, EACH HAVING A DISTINCT COLOR. IN MANY OF THE RITUALS IN THIS PACK WE WILL BE WORKING WITH THE CHAKRAS. EACH CHAKRA GOVERNS DIFFERENT EMOTIONS AND PARTS OF THE BODY, SO BY VISUALIZING AND MEDITATING ON THE CHAKRAS YOU CAN GREATLY INCREASE YOUR SELF-KNOWLEDGE.

OUR HIDDEN ENERGY SYSTEM

The chakra system is our own hidden energy system: tap into its power and you can keep yourself healthy, happy, and in perfect harmony. While scientists may insist that the chakras do not exist because they cannot be seen under the microscope, clairvoyants claim they can easily "see" the chakras. And a new development, the PIP scanner – which takes information from sound and light frequencies in the body – now manifests what the mystics have believed all along: the existence of oscillating spheres of energy in a vertical line down the body.

Chakras are precise monitors of our physical, emotional, and spiritual well-being. Each is said to spin at a different frequency, and, when each chakra spins at its optimum level, the body radiates perfect health; the emotions are centered and balanced and we enjoy happiness, health, and a deep sense of peace. It is a little like tuning into a radio station:

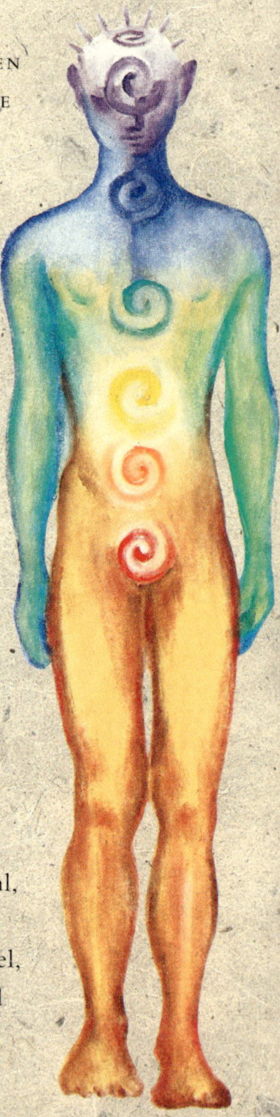

The chakra system is represented here by different spheres of color on the body. Chakras govern our spiritual, physical, and emotional well-being.

if you are on the wrong frequency the sound is distorted and unpleasant; once you hit the right frequency it becomes as clear as a bell. However, with all the stresses and strains of modern life it is easy for the chakras to fall out of frequency. When this happens we either feel under par, or we lose our emotional equilibrium. By working with the chakras regularly you can help bring them back into balance.

You can also use your chakras to "tune in" to various life issues. For example, if you want to connect to the feeling of unconditional love, you would focus on your heart chakra, visualizing it as a beautiful clear green wheel of energy, vibrating in your heart area.

THE CHAKRA SYSTEM

CHAKRA	LOCATION	COLOR	GOVERNS
Base	base of the spine	red	the physical body, social position
Genital	genitals	orange	sensuality, sexuality, emotions
Solar Plexus	solar plexus	yellow	self-esteem, energy, confidence, will, inner power
Heart	heart/chest	green	love, intimacy, balance, relationships
Throat	throat	blue	communication, creativity
Brow	forehead	indigo	imagination, intuition, dreams, and insights
Crown	top of the head	violet	understanding, connection with the divine

SELF-CLEARING

SMUDGING IS THE NAME GIVEN TO THE SACRED SMOKE BOWL BLESSING, A POWERFUL NATIVE NORTH AMERICAN CLEANSING TECHNIQUE. IT FORMS THE CENTRAL PART OF THE GREAT MAJORITY OF RITUALS AND BLESSINGS IN THIS BOOK. SMUDGING SUMMONS THE SPIRITS OF SACRED PLANTS, ASKING THEM TO DRIVE AWAY NEGATIVITY AND PUT YOU BACK INTO A STATE OF BALANCE. IT IS THE PSYCHIC EQUIVALENT OF WASHING YOUR HANDS BEFORE EATING AND IS USED AS AN ESSENTIAL PRELIMINARY TO ALMOST ALL NATIVE NORTH AMERICAN CEREMONIES.

you will need

- Smudge stick
- Matches
- Bowl or shell
- Large feather

INSTRUCTIONS

1. Light the end of your smudge stick (or bowl of smudge) and let it burn for a few minutes until the tip starts to smolder. You may need to fan the flames for a while. Then extinguish the flame so that the smudge stick smokes.

2. Call on the spirits of the smudge to cleanse and protect you, saying: "Sacred sage, drive away all negativity from my heart; take away everything unworthy and impure."

3. First waft the smoke toward your heart. Hold the smudge stick away from you and use the feather to waft the smoke toward you. Then take the smudge smoke over your head, down your arms, and down the front of your body. Imagine the smoke lifting away all the negative thoughts, emotions, and energies that have become attached to you.

After setting the smudge stick alight, fan the flames and then allow it to smolder.

4. Breathe in the smudge, visualizing the smoke purifying your body from within. (Note: be careful if you suffer from asthma or respiratory difficulties – experiment cautiously.)

5. Now bring the smoke down the back of your body toward the ground. Visualize the last vestiges of negativity being taken back into the earth, and away into the air.

6. Repeat your smudging once again, this time calling on the spirit of sweetgrass in this way: "Sacred sweetgrass, bring me the positive energy I need to do this work. Help me to become balanced. Purify my soul." As you smudge, imagine yourself being surrounded by gentle, loving energy – breathe in positivity, courage, and love.

SMUDGING SOMEONE ELSE

1. Use exactly the same technique to smudge someone else. Hold the bowl or smudge stick and waft the smoke over the person.

2. Ask the person to repeat the words after you. You might also want to ask if he or she feels any sense of blockage or uncomfortable feelings in any part of the body. If so, direct the smoke toward that area and ask the spirits of the smudge to help release the blockage, allowing energy to flow freely.

3. You may also direct smudge to each of the person's chakras: above the head; at brow level; at the throat; at the heart; at the solar plexus; at the genitals; and at the base of the spine. Visualize each chakra coming into balance as it is purified by the smudge.

As you waft the smoke from the smudge stick around your companion, ask him or her to repeat your words of blessing.

THE FOUR SPIRIT ANIMALS

IN NATIVE AMERICAN TRADITION, EVERYTHING IN CREATION – EVERY STONE, PLANT, AND ANIMAL – HAS A SPIRITUAL FORCE. THERE IS NO SENSE OF OURSELVES AND NATURE BEING SEPARATE: WE ARE ALL RELATIONS IN SPIRIT. SO CRYSTALS, HERBS, PLANTS, AND ANIMALS CAN BECOME OUR FRIENDS AND TEACHERS – AND SOME CAN BECOME POWERFUL TOTEMS OR ALLIES.

THE MEDICINE WHEEL

The Medicine Wheel forms an important part of Native North American tradition. It comprises a large ring of 36 stones laid out on the earth. Each stone represents a spiritual force – be it Father Sun, Mother Earth, or a series of totem animal spirits. By meditating on the Wheel or working with its symbols in ritual, it is possible to come to an understanding of the whole of creation and our own place within it. Unfortunately the entire Medicine Wheel is too complex to explore in a book of this size but we will be working with a very simplified version in our rituals.

The totem pole represents the ancestral heritage in Native North American tradition. The poles' designs often include animal spirits.

THE SPIRIT ANIMALS

The Medicine Wheel is like a giant compass. At each cardinal point, the directions North, South, East, and West, stands a Spirit Animal – the White Buffalo, Coyote, Eagle, and Grizzly Bear. Each of these totem animals is also connected with one of the four elements – Earth, Water, Air, and Fire.

Buffalo, Coyote, Eagle, and Bear are all strong guardians, and as you perform your smudging you can imagine the animals as large protective spiritual forces that will stand around you, protecting you at work.

You can also call on the energy of these great guardians whenever you need their particular attributes. So, if you are feeling stuck and need a solution, you could call on clever Coyote. If you are feeling frightened and need a powerful ally, ask for the help and protection of the great Grizzly Bear. When you need clear vision and insight, Eagle can come to your aid. Whenever you need grounding, the solid force of Buffalo can help.

There are variations on the animals and elements according to which tradition you follow, but these four are the most common and we refer to them in this pack.

The community house of Chief Kow-ish-te is decorated with an image of Grizzly Bear, one of the Spirit Animals.

DIRECTION	ANIMAL	ELEMENT	ATTRIBUTES
South	**Coyote**	**Water**	Clever, quick-minded – governs the emotions
West	**Bear**	**Fire**	Energetic, strong, powerful, determined – cleanses
East	**Eagle**	**Air**	Inspirational, far-sighted, fiercely protective – clarifies
North	**Buffalo**	**Earth**	Grounding, protective – gives knowledge of life and death

CONTACTING YOUR SPIRIT ANIMAL

ALTHOUGH YOU WILL PROBABLY COME TO LOVE AND HONOR ALL THE GREAT SPIRIT ANIMALS, YOU MAY FIND THAT YOU WILL FORM A SPECIAL RELATIONSHIP WITH ONE OF THESE POWERFUL GUARDIANS IN PARTICULAR. EQUALLY, YOU MAY DISCOVER THAT YOU HAVE OTHER ANIMAL ALLIES. AN ANIMAL ALLY OR SPIRIT ANIMAL CAN HELP ENORMOUSLY IN YOUR SMUDGE RITUALS AND IN YOUR LIFE. THIS SIMPLE RITUAL HELPS YOU CONNECT WITH YOUR OWN SPIRIT ANIMAL.

you will need

- Four stones
- Smudge stick
- Matches
- Bowl or shell
- Large feather

INSTRUCTIONS

1. Lay out four stones in a large diamond pattern. The stones represent the four great Spirit Animals: Buffalo ahead of you in the North; Coyote behind you to the South; Eagle to the East; and Bear to the West.

2. Light your smudge stick and smudge yourself, asking for cleansing and insight.

3. Sit quietly in the center of your Medicine Wheel and ground yourself. Feel yourself connected to the earth below and the sky above.

4. Feel your breathing become slow and regular. Become aware of your heart beating strongly and slowly.

5. Turn to face each direction and offer smudge to the guardian Spirit Animal of that direction, asking for insight and wisdom. Think about

Guardian Animal Spirit, cunning Coyote, decorates this traditional Native North American shield made of animal hide, wood, and feathers.

the qualities of that Spirit Animal. Do you share those qualities? Are they qualities that you would like to develop? Ask for help from each animal.

6. Now put your smudge to one side in its bowl or shell and lie down. Shut your eyes and imagine yourself lying in the center of a much larger Wheel, perhaps in some beautiful, natural place. Remember, beside each stone stands its guardian – Buffalo, Coyote, Eagle, and Bear.

7. Do you feel drawn to any particular animal? If so, visualize yourself walking up to the animal. Ask if you can talk to it. If it agrees, ask what you need to learn, politely requesting help and advice. Start to forge a friendship with "your" animal.

8. If none of the four Spirit Animals seems to call to you in this way, ask them if it is appropriate for you to meet your own spirit animal – you may well find that in response an animal or bird will appear. If so, ask if it is willing to help you. If nothing appears, don't worry, the time is not yet right.

9. If you have connected with an animal, ask if it will become your guide and protector in the smudging rituals you intend to carry out. If it agrees, give thanks – be very respectful.

10. Come back to waking reality and offer smudge in thanks to your own animal. Also offer smudge again to the four directions and their keepers.

As you meditate in your own Medicine Wheel, try to forge a friendship with one of the four animal guardians represented by the stones.

SPACE CLEARING

SMUDGING NOT ONLY CLEANSES PEOPLE; IT CAN ALSO CLEAR A ROOM OR AREA OF ANY OLD OR STAGNANT ENERGY. ALL ROOMS NEED CLEANSING, JUST AS MUCH AS THEY NEED PHYSICAL CLEANING. IF YOUR LIFE FEELS STUCK OR THINGS JUST AREN´T GOING ACCORDING TO PLAN, YOU MAY JUST FIND THAT SIMPLE SPACE CLEARING SOLVES THE PROBLEM. LEARNING ABOUT THE SPACE AROUND YOU IS ALSO AN IMPORTANT PART OF MOST RITUALS AND CEREMONIES.

you will need

- Smudge stick
- Matches
- Bowl or shell
- Large feather

INSTRUCTIONS

1. To cleanse the space in which you are working, light your smudge stick as described in the Self-Clearing ritual (see pages 16–17) and smudge yourself and anyone with you.

2. Walk around the room wafting smoke into each corner. Call on the spirit of sage to drive away negativity from the room. Then ask the spirit of sweetgrass to bring harmony and balance to the room.

3. Move to the center of the room and briefly stand still. Turn to the East of the room and fan smudge out into that direction four times, saying: "Spirit of the East, great Spirit of Air, cleanse and inspire this space."

4. Turn to the South and smudge four times, saying: "Spirit of the South, great Spirit of Water, strengthen and bring peace to this space."

It is important to enjoy your environment; smudging can cleanse a room of stagnant energy.

During this ceremony, you will address the spirits of North, South, East, and West.

5. Now turn to the West and smudge four times, saying: "Spirit of the West, great Spirit of Fire, energize and protect this space."

6. Turn to the North and smudge four times, saying: "Spirit of the North, great Spirit of Earth, ground and cleanse this space."

7. Return to your original position and look upward toward the heavens, this time sending smudge up in that direction four times. Say: "Great Father Sky, guard this space from above."

8. Finally, squat toward the floor and send smudge down to the earth four times, saying: "Great Mother Earth, nurture this space from below."

9. Put down your smudge stick and stand quietly with your eyes shut. Visualize the great spirits you have summoned standing guard around your room. You could imagine them as the great archangels or the four Spirit Animals of Native North American tradition (Buffalo – North; Eagle – East; Coyote – South; and Grizzly Bear – West). Visualize the loving energy of the mother and father spirits above and below you. Give thanks to all of them.

The healing properties of crystals will also benefit rooms in your house.

NOTE:
you should also smudge anything you will be using for your blessing, such as crystals, candles, flowers, or stones.

DEEP RELAXATION

RELAXATION IS THE KEY TO SMUDGING AND RITUAL WORK. YOU CANNOT PERFORM AN EFFECTIVE CLEANSING IF YOUR MIND IS WORRIED OR STRESSED. THIS TECHNIQUE CAN BE USED WHENEVER YOU WANT TO REACH A CALM, RELAXED STATE OF MIND; IT IS PARTICULARLY USEFUL IF YOU SUFFER FROM STRESS OR INSOMNIA.

you will need

- A comfortable couch, bed, or mat on the ground
- A blanket (if it's cold)

INSTRUCTIONS

1. Lie down and make yourself comfortable. Become aware of your breathing but don't attempt to alter it. Gently shut your eyes.

2. Become aware of your face and of any tension there. Now contract all the muscles in your face, quite forcefully, for one or two seconds. Then allow the muscles to relax completely.

3. Move now to your neck; tense and relax your neck muscles. Continue in the same way, traveling down through the shoulders and upper arms, the chest and back, and the lower arms and hands. Proceed down the body, concentrating on the abdomen, buttocks, thighs, calves, and feet.

4. If you are still feeling tense, repeat the process.

5. Now become aware of your body lying on the floor. Feel it connecting to the earth. Be grateful for the earth's support. Allow any remaining tension to drain away into the earth beneath you. Thank Mother Earth for absorbing your stress.

6. Imagine you are lying under a beautiful, warm but gentle sun. Feel the warmth of the sun's rays sinking softly into your body through every pore in your skin. Feel the warmth

The ancient Egyptians were well aware of the power of the sun's energy and its ability to benefit humankind. Here the god Osiris is represented sending rays of sun to his sister, the goddess Isis.

running gently through your body like liquid gold. Imagine the sun's healing power cleansing you and filling you with light and warmth. Appreciate the feeling of being supported by the earth and caressed by the sun.

7. Give thanks for your body and the wonderful job it does, and remind yourself to make time to keep it well nourished, exercised, and relaxed. Thank the earth and the sun for their loving support.

8. Gently stretch and open your eyes. Stamp your feet on the ground and shake yourself back to waking reality.

Allow the energizing rays of sunshine to warm your body.

NOTE:
you can use this technique to help you sleep: simply omit step 8 and allow yourself to fall into a deep, restful sleep.

AURA CLEANSING (VISUALIZATION)

THE AURA IS AN ELECTROMAGNETIC ENERGY FIELD THAT PERMEATES THE BODY AND EXTENDS SEVERAL FEET BEYOND IT. THE TECHNIQUE THAT FOLLOWS CLEARS THE AURA AND ALSO PROVIDES STRONG PROTECTION WHILE YOU ARE CONDUCTING CLEANSINGS AND BLESSINGS. IT IS PARTICULARLY USEFUL WHEN YOU CANNOT USE SMUDGE, PERHAPS BECAUSE YOU ARE AT WORK OR OUT AMONG PEOPLE.

you will need

- Just yourself!

INSTRUCTIONS

1. Stand or sit in a comfortable position. Spend a few moments focusing on your breathing and let it become comfortable and relaxed.

2. Think about the seven chakras – glowing energy centers located throughout your body (see pages 14–15). Imagine them pulsing through your body – feel the tingle of energy that they create.

3. Now let that energy extend out beyond your body so it forms a beautiful shimmering white bubble, egglike in shape, all around you. It goes right over your head and right under your feet. You are covered in front, behind, and on all sides.

4. Become aware of the strong protective quality of this bubble. No old, stale, expired energies can remain within it. No unwanted external energies can penetrate it. Yet you can easily send out your energy through it, and pleasant or wanted energy can enter your bubble.

5. Many people decide that their bubble is white but you can choose other colors if you prefer. Bright blue can be very purifying; a gentle green can be healing; and soft golden-pink can be very beautiful for spiritual work. Experiment and find out what suits you.

6. With practice you will be able to call up your bubble at will. It can be a very useful technique if you are on a bus or train; in a crowded place, or feeling uneasy at any time. Many people also like to use this technique before they go into an important meeting - or before they go to sleep.

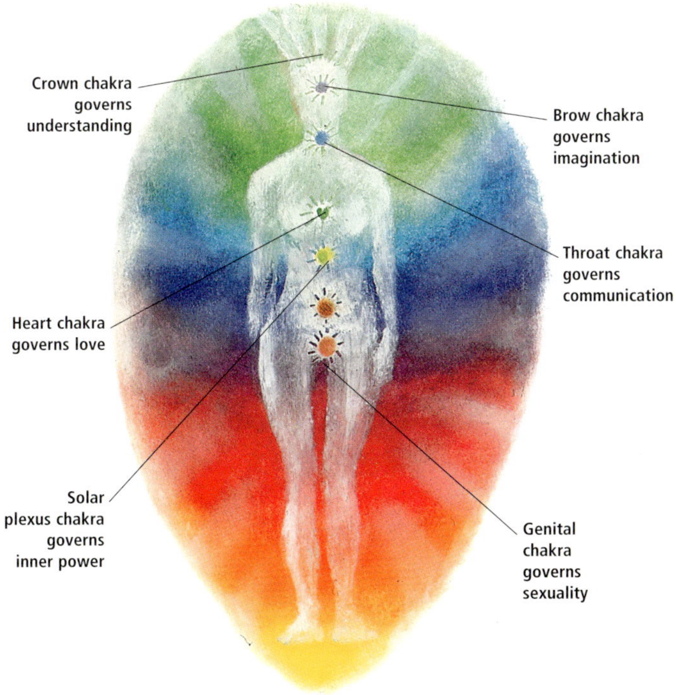

Our auras form a vibrant and protective bubble around ourselves. By meditating and visualizing our chakras, we can strengthen our auras.

MAKING A NEW SMUDGE STICK

ALTHOUGH SMUDGE STICKS ARE NOW READILY AVAILABLE FROM STORES SPECIALIZING IN NEW AGE AND NATIVE NORTH AMERICAN ARTIFACTS, YOU CAN EASILY MAKE YOUR OWN. CREATING YOUR OWN SMUDGE ALLOWS YOU TO FORGE A DEEPER CONNECTION WITH THE SPIRITS OF THE SACRED PLANTS USED IN SMUDGE, MAKING YOUR RITUALS AND CEREMONIES EVEN MORE MEANINGFUL.

On completion, your smudge stick should look something like this.

INSTRUCTIONS

1. If possible, you need to be able to pick your herbs fresh from the wild. Dried herbs will flare too easily. However, you can combine fresh and dried herbs if necessary.

2. Try to gather your herbs as they come into bloom during a waxing moon. Approach the plant with respect and ask its spirit for permission to use it in your smudge. Cut the plant with a sharp knife (you will need pieces around 8 to 12 inches long).

3. Gather your materials together and light the candle, asking the spirits of the plants you have gathered to help make powerful smudge.

4. Take a sturdy stick as a base. Arrange the other stems around it. Keep the dried herbs on the inside. Add the cornmeal or tobacco.

5. Take a piece of thread or animal hide and tie it around the stick, starting at the bottom.

you will need

- Selection of your chosen plants (see box)
- A sharp knife
- A sturdy stick
- Candle
- Matches
- A little tobacco or cornmeal
- Colored threads (embroidery threads work well) or animal hide

PLANTS TO USE IN SMUDGE STICKS

SAGEBRUSH

Confusingly, the sage most used in smudge sticks is not culinary sage but sagebrush; it transforms energy and brings change.

SAGE

You can also use culinary sage to bring wisdom and healing.

Sage

SWEETGRASS

Attracts positive energy. You can buy sweetgrass in braids – simply snip off a little for your smudge stick.

LAVENDER

Restores balance and creates a peaceful atmosphere. Lavender also attracts loving energy and spirits.

Lavender

CEDAR

Deeply purifying, especially useful for clearing negative emotion and healing.

Mugwort

MUGWORT

Stimulates psychic awareness and prophetic dreams. It also banishes evil spirits.

JUNIPER

Used to purify and create a safe and sacred space.

Juniper

YERBA SANTA

Used to purify and to set and protect boundaries.

Rosemary

ROSEMARY

A powerful healer that brings clarity.

If you want to add dried herbs that are powdered or crushed, you can put these on the inside of the smudge stick as you start to bind the bundle.

6. Tie your smudge stick quite firmly. The thread should reach at least halfway up the length of the stick.

7. Now hang your smudge stick by the tied end somewhere warm until it is almost dry, but not totally moisture-free.

MAKING A SACRED SMUDGE BOWL

NATIVE AMERICAN SHAMANS DO NOT ALWAYS USE SMUDGE STICKS; EQUALLY COMMON IS A LOOSE SMUDGE MIXTURE THAT IS PLACED IN A BOWL OR SHELL AND LIT. THIS IS EASY TO MAKE AND ESPECIALLY USEFUL IF YOU DO NOT HAVE ACCESS TO FRESH HERBS. IT ALSO HAS THE ADVANTAGE THAT, AS YOU BECOME MORE EXPERIENCED AND INTUITIVE, YOU CAN ALTER YOUR MIXTURE TO FIT EACH INDIVIDUAL RITUAL.

As an alternative to burning a smudge stick, you could burn the herbs of your choice in a shell.

INSTRUCTIONS

1. Sit down with all your ingredients. Light your candle and center yourself. You may like to carry out the Aura Cleansing ritual (see pages 26–27).

you will need

- Your choice of dried herbs and resins
- Bowl or shell
- Sea salt
- Self-igniting charcoal blocks
- Candle
- Matches
- Large feather

ADDITIONAL SMUDGE BOWL MIXES

Try the following for specific purposes:

Powerful cleansing mix (for clearing a new house): sage; sweetgrass; juniper.

Emotional cleansing mix (after arguments and in rituals relating to relationships): sage; cedar; lavender; borage (optional).

Mental clearing mix (when you need clarity): rosemary; juniper; tobacco (the pure leaves only); sweetgrass.

Healing mix (for sicknesses of both mind and body): sage; cedar; lavender; echinacea (optional).

Spiritual mix (for calling on the spirits, intuition, and divination): sage; mugwort; copal or frankincense (resins); lavender.

Ask the spirits of the plants you are using to give you their help in this ceremony.

2. Take a large shell or bowl able to withstand the heat of the burning charcoal. Ensure it is clean by washing it in water to which you have added a little sea salt.

3. A basic smudge mix would include a tablespoon of crumbled sage (either sagebrush or culinary sage) plus a teaspoon each of cedar bark and lavender. Mix the herbs together. See the box opposite for other ideas.

4. Place a charcoal block in your container and light it. Wait until the charcoal stops sparking and has turned white-gray.

5. Add a few pinches of your smudge mixture. It should readily smoke.

6. Use your smudge bowl in exactly the same way as you would your smudge stick – hold up the bowl and use the feather to direct smoke toward you or someone else, or out into the area in which you are working.

7. Add more smudge from time to time, as necessary.

You can use culinary sage to crumble into your smudge mixture.

USING CRYSTALS

CRYSTALS HAVE BEEN USED IN CEREMONIES ALL OVER THE WORLD FOR MILLENNIA. THEY ARE CONSIDERED TO BE STOREHOUSES OF POWER AND CAN HELP CONTAIN THE ENERGY SUMMONED UP IN A CEREMONY. CERTAIN KINDS OF CRYSTAL ALSO HAVE PARTICULAR QUALITIES. AS YOU BECOME MORE ACCUSTOMED TO PERFORMING RITUALS AND BLESSINGS YOU MAY WISH TO ENLIST THE HELPFUL POWERS OF ALTERNATIVE CRYSTALS. THE NEXT FOUR PAGES SHOW THE VARIETY AND USES OF DIFFERENT TYPES OF CRYSTAL.

Sodalite crystals, like the one above, are thought to affect the throat and brow chakras, helping communication and stablizing emotions.

YOUR TOTEM STONE

In Native North American tradition each crystal is linked with a particular spirit and used in ceremonies to help harness its power. Also, you may find that you are drawn to a particular stone or stones – this may well be your totem stone and can bring you knowledge and protection. It pays to sit quietly with such a stone, trying to sense your connection to it. Often you will be surprised at the results.

A crystal may be linked with a particular Animal Spirit, such as Great Buffalo.

HOW TO USE CRYSTALS

There are many ways of using crystals:

- You may wish to dedicate a particular stone to one purpose such as protecting your bedroom; helping you to concentrate at work; looking after a child; or protecting a room or the house.
- You can carry your chosen crystal around with you to imbue you with the powers of the stone.

• If you are healing a person, you may wish to place crystals on or around the body of your patient as you work.

• You can keep a crystal by you as you perform a ritual to augment the energy and to bring its particular powers to the ceremony.

you will need

- Crystal
- Warm water
- Sea salt
- Bowl
- Clean piece of cloth
- Smudge materials

INSTRUCTIONS

1. Cleanse your crystal by putting it in a solution of warm water and sea salt. Leave it for at least 36 hours and, if possible, for up to 70 hours. If you are able to do so, put it on a sunny ledge or out in the sun.

2. Once the cleansing time has elapsed, take your crystal from the water. Thank the salt and the water and pour it onto the earth. Gently dry your crystal with a clean piece of cloth.

A clean crystal is vital if you want to harness its full power. Cleanse your crystal in a bowl filled with warm water and sea salt.

3. Smudge yourself and your crystal (see pages 16–17).

4. Hold your crystal between your thumb and middle finger. Visualize your chakra located in your crown, at the top of your head – it is pulsing with energy. Bring that energy down toward your mouth and breathe it out in a sharp burst over the crystal. Now hold the crystal to your heart.

5. Say a short prayer or invocation, such as: "Bless this crystal and let it help me do good in my work." Choose words that fit the purpose of the crystal such as promoting a healing atmosphere, bringing serenity, or focusing the mind.

CHOOSING YOUR CRYSTALS

CRYSTALS ARE HEALING STONES BUT HAVE VARIOUS ADDITIONAL POWERS. HUGE NUMBERS OF CRYSTALS ARE AVAILABLE. THE ONES ILLUSTRATED ON THESE PAGES ARE PROBABLY THE MOST USEFUL, PARTICULARLY AS YOU BEGIN YOUR WORK. WHEN YOU CHOOSE A CRYSTAL, YOU SHOULD BE UNCONSCIOUSLY DRAWN TO THE RIGHT CRYSTAL FOR YOU. IT MAY NOT BE THE SHAPE OR SIZE YOU HAD IMAGINED BUT TRUST YOUR INTUITION – THAT STONE WAS MEANT FOR YOU!

THE STONES

QUARTZ: Clear quartz crystals are power stones. They amplify, transmit, and receive energy. Quartz can also help bring you clarity and a sense of true purpose – it can help you balance your chakras.
USE IT: In all ceremonies and rituals. A powerful, general-purpose stone.

Quartz

TURQUOISE: A beautiful protective stone, believed by Native North Americans to keep the owner from danger. Turquoise is a great healer and can strengthen you after illness or in times of need. It also promotes success and fulfillment.
USE IT: In healing ceremonies; carry it with you or wear jewelry with turquoise incorporated into it.

Turquoise

AMETHYST: Amethyst is a soothing and cleansing stone. It can help you meditate and will promote a good night's sleep. Native North American lore says it teaches discrimination and will help put you in touch with the source of any anger.

Amethyst

USE IT: In nighttime rituals; keep it by your bedside as you sleep. For any ritual where you need a calm, reasoned atmosphere. For meditation and rituals of self-knowledge.

Sodalite

SODALITE: A positive, balancing stone, sodalite helps with cleansing on all levels – physical, mental, emotional, and spiritual. In Native North American tradition it is said to keep the spirit cleansed and the heart pure.

USE IT: For all cleansing rituals, both self-clearing and space cleansing. Use it when you want to release negative emotions. It can also be useful for healing rituals.

Citrine

CITRINE: Citrine clears the mind; it gives confidence and optimism. It can foster friendship and help dispel fear. It is also said to be a "money" stone, conferring wealth to the individual and bringing affluence into the house.

USE IT: For start-of-the-day rituals and any ceremonies to bring prosperity and abundance. Anyone taking a test or exam should carry citrine with them.

Rose Quartz

ROSE QUARTZ: This delicate pink stone is a beautiful symbol of love and peace – it is the stone of harmony. It promotes self-esteem and helps to heal grief. It also resonates with the family and children in particular.

USE IT: In rituals in which you want to foster love and peace. It can be helpful and healing when someone close to you dies. Dedicate a piece of rose quartz to guard a nursery or children's room.

USING ESSENTIAL OILS

ESSENTIAL OILS ADD A DELICIOUS, SWEET-SMELLING ELEMENT TO RITUALS AND BLESSINGS. YOU CAN COMBINE THEIR USE WITH SMUDGING OR USE THEM ON OCCASIONS WHEN IT WOULD NOT BE SUITABLE TO USE YOUR SMUDGE STICK. ESSENTIAL OILS CAN ALSO EXTEND THE EFFECTIVENESS OF THE ATMOSPHERE SUMMONED BY YOUR RITUALS, AS THE SCENT OF THE OILS CAN LINGER FOR HOURS.

To fill a room with the scent of the essential oil of your choice, heat it in an oil burner.

AN ANCIENT AROMATIC TRADITION

The healing power of plants has been used by many cultures for thousands of years – from India to Egypt; from Greece and Rome to Europe and the Americas. Far back in prehistory, it was recognized that burning different plants, their woods or oils, produced a variety of effects: promoting well-being, healing the sick, and inducing spiritual experiences. Smudging is one example of this practice, the burning of aromatherapy oils, another.

HOW TO USE ESSENTIAL OILS

In this book we recommend that you vaporize essential oils in a burner or bowl of warm water; this releases their healing scents. An individual oil can even have a stimulating effect on one part of the body while sedating another. However, there are other ways of incorporating essential oils into your rituals. As you become more experienced you might like to consider using oils in the following way:

• In the bath: adding essential oils to your bath can turn your bathroom into a sacred space and transform bathing into a ritual. Add four to six drops of oil and make sure you swish the water around. Alternatively, make your own bath oil mix by combining three tablespoons of sweet almond or avocado oil with 20 drops of your chosen oil or oils. Add one teaspoon to your bath.

• In a massage blend: massage is a powerful way of using oils because you inhale the aromatic molecules and absorb them through your skin. You could incorporate it as part of a nighttime ritual (such as Consecrating Your Bedroom ritual on pages 48–49). A massage is a perfect way to begin or end the ceremony. Mix six drops of your chosen oil or oils with four teaspoons of sweet almond or apricot kernel oil.

• On a kleenex: Often it can be difficult to use your smudge stick or even to burn essential oils because you may be at work or away from home. But you can still use the power of scent and the helpful plant spirits. Simply put a few drops of your chosen oil on a kleenex or handkerchief and sniff the scent. This is also useful as a quick pick-me-up.

CAUTION

Essential oils are powerful medicine. Never exceed the stated amount and do not take internally or undiluted on your skin unless under the supervision of a qualified practitioner or physician. Some oils should not be taken during pregnancy or if you suffer from epilepsy. Check with your doctor.

Massage, using aromatic oils, provides healing and relaxation. The same effects can be achieved by burning oils.

CHOOSING YOUR ESSENTIAL OILS

THERE ARE SO MANY ESSENTIAL OILS THAT IT CAN BE HARD TO KNOW WHICH TO PICK. IN THIS BOOK WE USE MAINLY LAVENDER, PLUS A FEW OTHER READILY AVAILABLE OILS. BUT ONE OF THE GREAT JOYS OF AROMATHERAPY IS EXPERIMENTING WITH DIFFERENT OILS AND BLENDS. AS A GENERAL RULE, THE OILS YOU NEED ARE THE ONES TO WHICH YOU ARE DRAWN. TEST OUT A FEW AND IMAGINE HOW YOU COULD INCORPORATE THEM INTO YOUR RITUALS AND EVERYDAY LIFE. REMEMBER, YOUR INTUITION WILL SERVE YOU WELL.

A STARTER SELECTION

Lavender is well known for its soothing qualities.

LAVENDER: One of the most generally useful oils that can be used in a huge array of rituals. Lavender is healing, purifying, balancing, and soothing. It gives resolution in difficult times and helps to release negative emotions. It can ease stress and aid peaceful sleep, so use it in all rituals where you want a calm, relaxed, and healing atmosphere.

GERANIUM: Geranium is the "feelgood" oil – it balances the emotions, lifts depression, and makes you feel uplifted yet relaxed. According to folklore geranium can keep away evil spirits. Geranium works well blended with lavender when you want a calm yet happy atmosphere – for family gatherings or children's parties, perhaps.

Geranium balances emotion.

SANDALWOOD: Sandalwood has been considered sacred for thousands of years: in the East it was used as an aid to meditation, to soothe anxiety and insomnia, and even to speed the souls of the dead to heaven. It is very soothing and can be used instead of lavender in bathtime and bedtime blessings. Because sandalwood helps release the past and encourages transition, it is ideal for use in rituals commemorating the dead.

Citrus oils refresh us and help us to let go.

GRAPEFRUIT, LEMON, ORANGE: Citrus oils are all wonderful for lifting the spirits. They are bright, cheery, stimulating oils that work well as party oils and for enlivening the home. Also think of these oils when you want to deal with stress but need to keep alert; they are great balancers. Lemon helps us to accept change and let go, so it is very useful in rituals of releasing and separation.

JUNIPER: Juniper is a deeply cleansing and protective oil, so eminently suited to most rituals. It is sometimes added to smudge sticks or mixtures. Juniper stimulates the mind so can be useful if you are studying or working hard. It helps raise self-esteem and can support you in difficult times.

TEA TREE: Tea tree is a friend in need if you want to keep yourself or your home free from infection. It is a powerful antifungal, antiviral, and antibacterial oil that makes it a practical ally in any healing or sickroom cleansings.

YLANG-YLANG: Ylang-ylang is a renowned aphrodisiac so invaluable in any rituals involving love or sex. It is also soothing and calming, so use it in bedtime blessings or in party blends. Ylang-ylang promotes confidence too.

CHAPTER ONE
HOME BLESSINGS

OUR HOMES ARE LIVING ENTITIES – FAR MORE THAN MERE BRICKS AND MORTAR, OR WOOD AND PLASTER. A HOME CONTAINS A SPIRIT AND A SOUL, JUST AS YOU DO. THE RITUALS AND BLESSINGS IN THIS CHAPTER ALLOW YOU TO CONNECT WITH THE SPIRIT OF YOUR HOME, TURNING IT INTO A PLACE OF COMFORT AND RENEWAL; A WELCOMING REFUGE FROM THE STRESSES AND STRAINS OF EVERYDAY LIFE.

THE UNSEEN ENERGY IN OUR HOMES

Guatemalans prepare to enter a new home with a religious procession.

Most of us tend to think of our homes as walls, roof, floor, and furniture. Yet our homes are also made of energy that is constantly shifting, moving, and changing. This is the subtle energy of the home and it is affected by the atmosphere and mood of the people within it. Sometimes we walk into a house and just feel that it is wrong – the atmosphere is desperately uncomfortable. This happens when houses are left for years without any form of psychic cleansing. Imagine if you hadn't physically cleaned your home for years – no dusting, no vacuuming, and no window cleaning. It would be filthy. Now think about what has gone on in, say your living room, over the last ten years, or even the last year! There will hopefully have been good times, but equally you might have had arguments, felt angry, depressed, or sad. Other people could have brought in their troubles and woes (and left behind their negative energy).

THE ANCIENT HISTORY OF SPACE CLEANSING

In cultures where this concept of vital energy is understood and honored, people spend as much time on psychic cleansing as they do bathing and washing their physical bodies. You will find versions of space cleansing as far afield as Hawaii and Bali, China and Siberia, and India and the Middle East. The ancient Native North American cultures understood that all forms of life are inherently based on energy – the universe is not fixed and static, but in constant flux and movement. Their smudge ceremony was precisely designed to cleanse the energetic aura of the ritual area. Nowadays the use of smudging has been extended to cleanse and balance the energy in our everyday homes.

This nineteenth-century wood engraving depicts Native North Americans performing a ritual dance outside their home.

BECOMING AWARE OF SUBTLE ENERGY

THE FIRST STEP TOWARD SUCCESSFUL SMUDGING AND SPACE CLEANSING IS TO BECOME AWARE OF SUBTLE ENERGY – BOTH IN OURSELVES AND IN THE ATMOSPHERE. THIS IS A PROCESS YOU CAN LEARN QUITE EASILY, AND, WITH A LITTLE PRACTICE AND DEDICATION, YOU SHOULD SOON BECOME ADEPT AT SENSING SUBTLE ENERGY.

You can sense energy within yourself by holding your hands slightly apart and bouncing them toward each other.

SENSING ENERGY IN YOURSELF

1. Choose a time when you can be quiet and alone – this exercise requires a peaceful environment and concentration. Wash your hands and take off any rings, bracelets, watches, or any other accessories.

2. Sit down with your hands resting on your lap, palms facing upward. Close your eyes.

3. Relax your hands and focus your attention on your palms. Turn your palms to face each other, hold them about 18 inches apart. Slightly curve them as if you were holding a soft ball. You may well feel a warmth or a tingling between your hands – that is subtle energy.

4. Bounce your palms toward each other as if you were gently squeezing and releasing the invisible ball. Feel the energy shift as you move – it may feel like a cool breeze. Imagine the ball gently expanding until it reaches the size of a beach ball.

5. Now bring your palms together as if you were holding a tennis ball. Ask yourself whether the energy feels any different.

Hold your hand about six inches above your pet's fur and see if you can sense its energy.

SENSING ENERGY ELSEWHERE

You can swiftly learn to feel energy in the house. Start by practicing on animals and plants. Try "stroking" a cat or dog with your fingers about six inches away from it – feel its energy. Try putting your hands over a living plant – sense the energy. Now compare it with the energy given off by a bunch of fresh flowers; learn to detect the subtle differences.

From here you could progress to sensing the energy in objects around the home. See if you can detect the difference between a handcrafted object and a mass-produced one. If you become adept, you may find you can tell the history of an object. This practice, called psychometry, is used by psychics.

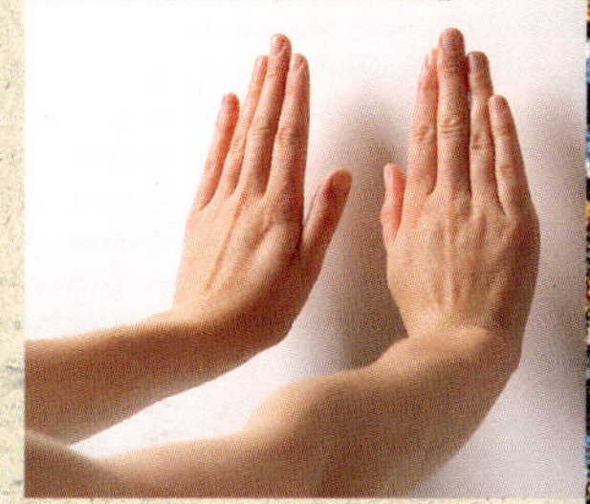

Try to sense energy in a room before you smudge it.

SENSING ENERGY IN THE HOME

1. Start at the entrance of the room and hold your hand a few inches from the wall in a motion that is similar to stroking a dog.

2. Be sensitive and concentrate, "listening" with your hand for the energy. You may find some areas are quite calm and smooth; others will be disturbed, stuck, or stale. Talk to the house and reassure it that you are going to cleanse and purify it to release it from any negativity.

3. When you return to the entrance, make a note of any stuck areas. These are where you will need to direct the most energy when you smudge the room.

BLESSING YOUR NEW HOME

THIS CLEANSING BLESSING CLEARS THE ATMOSPHERE OF OLD STAGNANT ENERGY. USE IT WHENEVER YOU MOVE INTO A NEW HOME AND AT LEAST ONCE A YEAR AFTER THAT. IT WILL LEAVE YOUR HOME FEELING FRESH, COMFORTING, AND ENERGIZED.

you will need

- Smudge stick
- Matches
- Bowl or shell
- Large feather
- Candle and holder
- Lavender oil and a burner or bowl of hot water

INSTRUCTIONS

1. Collect everything you need at the center of your home. Remove your shoes and any jewelry. Light your smudge stick and smudge yourself and those items you will be using. Leave your smudge smoking in its bowl.

2. Quietly center yourself and think about your purpose in blessing your home. Say: "I call upon the guardians of the elements, of Earth, Fire, Water, and Air, to help me cleanse this home." (Or substitute your own prayer.) Wait for a moment and feel the presence of these four great guardians lovingly surrounding you.

Remember to take off your jewelry before starting the cleansing ritual.

3. Light your candle, saying: "I light the fire that glows in the heart of the home. May peace be here."

4. Go around the house, smudging each room. Say:

All the elements – Earth, Fire, Water, and Air – are called upon to cleanse a new home.

"Cleansing power of the spirits of the smoke, drive away all negativity. Bless this home and bring it joy and laughter." Walk back to the center of the house. Light your oil burner or fill the bowl with hot water. Take the lavender oil and let seven drops fall into the water, saying: "May this home be a haven from the world." Imagine the scent of the lavender, mingling with the smudge, carrying joy, security, and a profound sense of peace throughout your home.

5. Stand quietly for a moment. Look at the candle and bring your hands toward your heart (as if you were taking the flame inside) saying: "Let the protective flame burn steadily in the heart of my home."

6. Softly blow out the candle. Put out your smudge, thanking the spirits of the smudge for their help. Finally, say a word of grateful thanks to the guardian spirits.

SHIELDING YOUR HOME

WE ALL WANT TO FEEL SAFE AND SECURE IN OUR HOMES. THIS IS A POWERFUL PROTECTIVE RITUAL THAT TURNS YOUR HOME INTO A KIND OF SPIRITUAL FORTRESS. USE THIS RITUAL WHENEVER YOU FEEL THE NEED – MAYBE LAST THING AT NIGHT OR WHEN YOU LEAVE THE HOUSE – AND PARTICULARLY IF YOU ARE GOING AWAY ON A LONG TRIP.

you will need

- Smudge stick
- Matches
- Bowl or shell
- Large feather

INSTRUCTIONS

1. Stand in the center of your home. Sense the energy of your environment, then smudge yourself and cleanse your aura (see pages 26–27).

2. Expand your bubble of protection until it fills the entire building. Move to the East corner of your home. Visualize yourself holding a beautiful, bright sword of light between your hands. It is like a light-saber shown in the movie *Star Wars*, sending out a beam of pure energy.

3. Visualize a huge guardian figure behind you – this is the great Eagle Spirit. Imagine yourself, with a sweep of your arm, pushing a forcefield of energy into the ground beneath you. Say: "Great Eagle, Spirit of Air, protect the East."

4. Do the same in the South corner of your home. This time summon clever Coyote. Bring down the forcefield of energy, saying: "Great Coyote, Spirit of Water, protect the South."

Native North Americans decorated their totem poles with Animal Spirits such as Great Eagle. Totem poles are representative of individual tribes and their ancestors.

Figure out the bearings of your own house before calling on the spirits to protect it.

5. Now shift to the West where you will summon the power of the fierce Grizzly Bear. Bring down the forcefield of energy, saying: "Great Bear, Spirit of Fire, protect the West."
6. Finally move to the North where you summon the protection of Earth and the powerful Buffalo Spirit. As you bring down the forcefield of energy, ask: "Great Buffalo, Spirit of Earth, protect the North."
7. Now visualize the four forcefields of shimmering energy merging together to create a safe haven. If you like, you can ask the four guardian animals to stay and guard their corners.
8. Respectfully thank the powers for their help. Your home should now be safe.

NOTE:
if you are going away from home for some time you may have to visualize even further. If you have someone coming in to look after a cat or plants, you will need to visualize that person entering and leaving without disturbing your forcefield.

CONSECRATING YOUR BEDROOM

YOUR BEDROOM SHOULD BE A PLACE OF REST AND REFUGE, SOMEWHERE YOU CAN RELAX AFTER A HARD DAY'S WORK. THIS LOVELY BLESSING CALLS ON YOUR GUARDIAN ANGEL TO CONSECRATE YOUR BEDROOM.

you will need

- Smudge stick
- Matches
- Bowl or shell
- Large feather
- White candle
- Lavender oil plus a burner or bowl of hot water
- Some pebbles
- Rose quartz crystal (optional)

INSTRUCTIONS

1. Sit in the center of the room and breathe quietly and calmly. Smudge yourself, the items you are using, and the room.

2. Light your candle and say: "May my guardian angel come near and bring love and peace to this room." You might have a sense of a divine, loving being embracing you with its soft wings.

3. Let five drops of lavender oil fall into the water of your burner or bowl. As each drop hits the water imagine a spark of loving energy (like a tiny fairy) flying out from the oil to each corner of the room. The last drop's energy shoots to the center of the room. Imagine your angel smiling with pleasure at the lavender spirits.

4. Ask the gentle spirits of the lavender to bring you peace, rest, relaxation, and sweet dreams.

5. Perform the Aura Cleansing ritual (see pages 26–27), but this time fill your aura with a beautiful soft pinkish-gold color. Let that soft-colored light expand beyond your aura to embrace the entire room.

Imagine your pebbles imbued with the pink-gold light of your aura.

YOUR BEDROOM CRYSTAL

You could also decide to dedicate a crystal as your bedroom guardian. A rose quartz is excellent for this purpose. Make sure you have cleansed it. During the bedroom consecration, ask your guardian angel to bless the crystal. You can also visualize it imbued with the pink-gold light. Keep it by your bedside or on your dressing table.

By keeping a crystal in your bedroom as a guardian you can enjoy a deep and refreshing sleep.

6. Hold some pebbles in your hand and imagine them, too, imbued with the pink-gold light. Place one in each corner of the room to hold the love and light intact throughout your space.
7. Thank your guardian angel. You may also ask for any particular blessing or protection. In return envisage a flame of pure love shooting from your heart to your angel.
8. Softly blow out the candle and the oil burner, if you are using one. If you have chosen a bowl of hot water it can be left in place.

SICKROOM CLEANSING

IF SOMEONE IN THE HOUSE IS SICK, THIS IS A DELIGHTFUL CLEANSING WHICH WILL HELP LIFT THEIR SPIRITS AND ALSO BANISH BUGS SO THAT OTHER MEMBERS OF THE FAMILY STAY HEALTHY!

you will need

- Smudge stick
- Matches
- Bowl or shell
- Large feather
- Candle
- White cloth
- Oill Burner
- Lavender and tea tree oil
- Crystal (cleansed)
- Flowers (optional)

INSTRUCTIONS

1. Prepare for the cleansing by smudging yourself (if the smoke irritates your patient, do this away from the sickroom).

2. Set up an "altar" in the sickroom. It could be a table, shelf, or window ledge. Cover it with a clean white cloth and on top of the cloth place your oil burner, crystal, and the candle (make sure it is in a bowl of water or sand so that it is not hazardous). You could also add a bunch of fresh flowers, providing the pollen doesn't irritate your patient.

3. Light both the candle and your oil burner and add four drops each of lavender and tea tree oil. As you do so, call on the Great Buffalo Spirit (who rules physical healing). Imagine Buffalo's gentle healing power embracing the room.

4. Hold up your crystal and ask for the healing power of the earth and the sky to come into the crystal and to hold the healing energy in this room. Imagine the energy coming into the crystal and feel it tingling in your body.

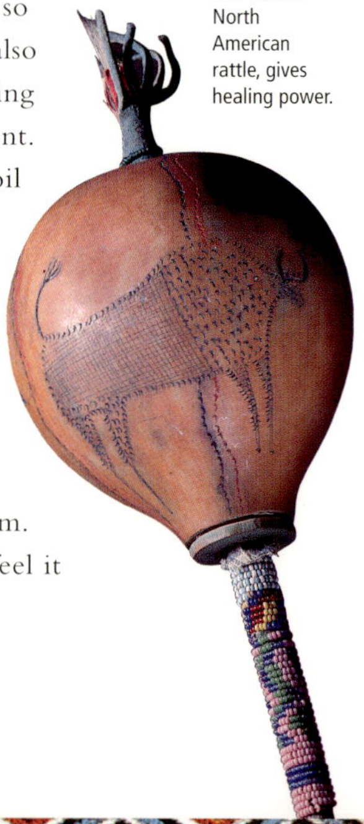

The Great Buffalo Spirit, depicted on this Native North American rattle, gives healing power.

When someone is ill in bed, you can offer them a spirit-lifting blessing.

5. Ask the patient to relax. Read them the instructions for the Aura Cleansing ritual, (see pages 26–27), and ask them to imagine the light bringing them relaxation, healing and comfort.

6. Thank Buffalo for his help and ask him to protect your patient and the sickroom.

Fresh flowers will fill a sickroom with a pleasant aroma.

CLEANSING FOLLOWING AN ARGUMENT

IT HAPPENS TO ALL OF US. YOU´VE HAD A TERRIBLE ARGUMENT OR AN UNPLEASANT TIFF AND NOW YOU´RE FEELING TERRIBLE; THE ATMOSPHERE IN THE ROOM IS SO THICK YOU COULD CUT IT WITH A KNIFE. THIS CLEANSING CAN RESTORE TRANQUILLITY TO YOUR ROOM AND MAY EVEN PROVIDE THE IMPETUS FOR A RECONCILIATION AND RETURN TO HAPPINESS.

you will need

- Smudge stick
- Matches
- Bowl or shell
- Large feather
- Party squeaker
- Plant mister with a few drops of Rescue Remedy from the Bach Flower Remedies added to the water (optional)

INSTRUCTIONS

1. First you need to smudge yourself and, if possible, the person with whom you've had the argument. Ask the spirits of the smudge to cleanse you of your bad feelings towards the person with whom you've argued.

2. Take the smudge around the room, wafting it into each corner (use the feather if you like). Ask the spirits of the smudge to take away all the negativity and bad feelings that have been unleashed in the room.

3. Stand quietly in the center of the room and ask Coyote who governs relationships to provide you with deeper knowledge and understanding about the causes of your fight. Don't judge or interrupt, just listen.

4. Even if you still feel you were in the right, send unconditional love to the person with whom you've argued. Imagine love

Fill a plant mister with Rescue Remedy diluted with water and use it in this cleansing ritual.

coming from your heart chakra to theirs. Send forgiveness. This action is incredibly powerful and transforming.

5. Now it's time to shift the atmosphere of the room. Take your squeaker and blow it noisily around the room – this sounds frivolous but it really moves the energy, bringing renewal.

6. If you like you can finish by spraying the room with the plant mister and Rescue Remedy.

Negative energy between two people can often stay behind in a room. Use this cleansing ritual to lighten the atmosphere after an argument.

Clever Coyote, depicted in this native North American headdress, should be called upon to help in this ritual.

LEAVING YOUR HOME

LEAVING A HOME CAN BE A TERRIBLE WRENCH. HOWEVER MUCH YOU ARE LOOKING FORWARD TO MOVING INTO YOUR NEW SPACE, YOUR OLD HOME WILL UNDOUBTEDLY HOLD MANY FOND MEMORIES. YOU NEED A RITUAL TO ENSURE THAT YOUR MOVE GOES SMOOTHLY AND THAT YOU LEAVE THE PLACE IN A FIT STATE FOR THE NEW OCCUPANTS.

you will need

- Smudge stick
- Matches
- Bowl or shell
- Large feather
- Two candles

Looking at old photo albums can help revive fond memories of past times

INSTRUCTIONS

1. Smudge yourself.

2. Stand quietly in the center of your home and try to sense the spirit of your home. Explain to it that you are moving and would like to invite it to join you.

3. Light your first candle and place it in the center of your home. Say to your house spirit: "Spirit of the home, please fill this flame with all the joy and good memories that we have from this room. Let them come down into this candle."

Leaving home can be both exciting and disruptive; this ceremony helps you prepare yourself for the change.

4. Sit quietly and remember all the good times you have had in your home. Bring those memories into the candle flame; imagine them glowing at the center of the flame.

5. When you feel you have pulled in all your good memories, invite the spirit of your home to come down into the candle and accompany you to your new home. Blow out the candle.

6. Smudge the whole house carefully to leave it clean and clear for its new owners.

7. When you have safely arrived at your new home, light your second candle, saying: "May peace, prosperity, happiness, health, and laughter fill this house."

8. Light your old home candle from the new one. Place them alongside each other in the heart of your new home and visualize your familiar home spirit blending into its new home. Once the candles have burned down, set aside time to perform the Blessing Your New Home ritual, (see pages 44–45).

These two candles represent your old and new homes.

NOTE:
it used to be common practice to bring a smoldering log from the fire in your old home to light the fire in your new home. Try it for yourself!

CHAPTER TWO
FAMILY BLESSINGS

FAMILY BLESSINGS AND CEREMONIES HELP TO BOND A FAMILY TOGETHER. THEY BRING US CLOSE DURING PIVOTAL TIMES OF OUR LIVES AND HELP GIVE MEANING TO WHAT CAN BE CONFUSING OR DIFFICULT PERIODS. EQUALLY, SIMPLE RITUALS CAN MAKE FAMILY LIFE FAR MORE FUN – INVOLVE ALL THE FAMILY AND WATCH THE ATMOSPHERE IN YOUR HOME TRANSFORM!

Time together for the family is often hard to organize but vital to everyone's well-being.

THE IMPORTANCE OF RITUAL FOR THE FAMILY

We already have family rituals, or vestiges of them: we gather around a font to welcome a baby into the world; we join together to say goodbye to people when they die; family and friends travel great distances to attend weddings; and we blow out the candles on a birthday cake.

But often our present-day ceremonies seem lacking in the power to comfort or inspire. We seem to go through the motions. We focus on the exterior values (clothes, food, and etiquette) and seem to lose track of the ritual's inner meaning.

A good ritual helps us to make sense of life's events. It can help to put us in touch with deep feelings and give us an outlet for negative or difficult emotions. The rituals in this chapter are not intended to take the place of normal practice, but can be seen as a useful addition. Often we do not even have public ceremonies for difficult occasions such as separation or divorce, yet cutting the ties can be an essential part of moving on in life.

DESIGNING YOUR OWN RITUALS

The rituals in this chapter are not all linked to momentous life events. Ideas for a simple birthday blessing and a mood-enhancing cleansing to perform before a party are included. Rituals like this are fun – they help proceedings go with a bang!

The very best rituals are those that have depth and meaning for you and your family. Take some time before the event to think about what you want. Discuss it with your family, taking the ideas in this book as a starting point. If you are planning a birthday celebration you might want to include something for the birthday person: a game; favorite stories or poems; or you could make cutting the cake part of your ritual.

All sorts of events, such as birthdays, weddings, and marriages, can be marked with smudge blessings of your own invention.

If you are planning a party, why not invite a few of your closest friends around early to help you with your ritual? The energy of several people will liven up the atmosphere. Above all, enjoy your family rituals. If they aren't meaningful or fun, they aren't serving their purpose. Give your intuition and imagination free rein.

BIRTHDAY BLESSING

A BIRTHDAY IS A PIVOTAL POINT IN YOUR PERSONAL YEAR. MAKE IT SPECIAL WITH THIS SIMPLE RITUAL, WHICH CAN BE USED AS A SOLO CEREMONY OR INCORPORATED INTO A SOCIAL GATHERING.

you will need

- Candle
- Smudge stick
- Matches
- Bowl or shell
- Large feather
- Crystal (freshly cleansed)

INSTRUCTIONS

1. Sit down quietly (if you have people with you, let them form a circle with you in the center). Light your candle and as you watch its flame remember the past year.

2. Think of all the good things that happened, the high points and low points – any major challenges. If you are in a group you may wish to remember these out loud. Then ask other people to add their thoughts and memories of your year – important events such as fun outing and little things you might have said.

3. Thank the Great Spirit for the gift of your life in the year that has passed and for all the joys and lessons it brought. Summon Buffalo, who teaches acceptance and forgiveness, and say: "I thank the old year and release it with joy. Now I look forward to the new."

Birthdays are not only a time for receiving gifts; they are also a celebration of the past year.

4. Smudge yourself and (if you have company) your friends and family, consciously releasing any negativity from the past year. Be aware that this is a new start – a fresh beginning, full of opportunity.

5. Smudge your crystal too and dedicate it to the new year, saying: "May this new year in my life bring me..." (choose carefully your wishes for your next year). Other people may also like to give you wishes or encouragement for the year ahead.

Sometimes it is good to write down your hopes and plans for the year to come.

6. You may find it helpful to write down your hopes and wishes for the year ahead and keep them recorded as inspiration should you need it.

7. After this quiet time, proceed with your usual celebrations!

Friends often make a birthday celebration magical; try to include them in this birthday blessing.

BEFORE THE PARTY MOOD ENHANCER

YOU NEED MORE THAN GOOD MUSIC, FOOD, AND DRINK FOR A GREAT PARTY. YOU NEED A WELCOMING, RELAXED, AND HAPPY ATMOSPHERE. PREPARE YOUR PARTY ROOM (OR ROOMS) WITH THIS FUN RITUAL.

you will need

- Smudge stick
- Matches
- Bowl or shell
- Large feather
- Drums, rattles, or lively music
- Orange and yellow candles (in pots of sand or water)
- Essential oils (grapefruit, lemon, orange are ideal) and burner

INSTRUCTIONS

1. Smudge yourself and the main rooms in which you will hold your party. Leave the smudge to burn quietly for a while.

2. Start drumming or put on some music with a strong rhythm. Start to dance. Shut your eyes and feel the beat of the music. Smell the smudge and ask Coyote, who loves fun and parties, to connect you with the music.

3. As you dance, feel your connection with the people who will be coming to join your party. Imagine them having fun, laughing, dancing, and talking. Ask the spirits to bring joy and delight to your gathering. If you have a personal Spirit Animal ask it to join you in the dance and to bring the fun, lighthearted aspect of its personality to your party.

You need a drum, a rattle, or rhythmic music to enhance your mood before a party.

4. When you feel the atmosphere start to enliven, bring yourself back to normal awareness and open your eyes.
5. Put out your smudge, thanking the spirits for their help.
6. Light your candles and aromatherapy oils and leave them to burn through your party, making sure they are in a safe place. The oils suggested here are energizing and joyful - if you would prefer a peaceful atmosphere, use lavender instead.
7. Enjoy yourself!

Dancing at a party really helps you to let your hair down. To get in the mood for a party, try this ritual, which releases inhibitions and connects you to those around you.

CELEBRATING A BIRTH

THE BIRTH OF A BABY IS A MIRACULOUS EVENT, WORTHY OF GREAT CELEBRATION. WHETHER OR NOT YOU INTEND A FORMAL RELIGIOUS CEREMONY, THIS GENTLE BLESSING IS A LOVELY WAY TO WELCOME A NEW SOUL INTO THE WORLD.

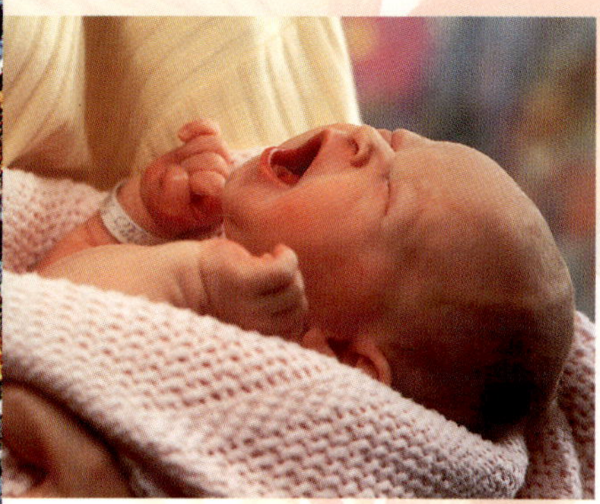

The birth of a baby is one of the most miraculous events of our lives.

you will need

- Table or cloth
- Smudge stick
- Matches
- Bowl or shell
- Large feather
- Candle
- Bowl of water
- Salt
- Flower petals
- Crystal (cleansed)

INSTRUCTIONS

1. Set your ingredients on a table or on a cloth on the ground. If the weather is fine, it is lovely to perform this blessing outdoors.

2. Light your smudge. Smudge yourself, and the people around you. Then smudge the baby, keeping the smoke out of his or her eyes.

3. Place the baby on the earth and say: "Mother Earth, love and protect this young one."

4. Pick up the baby and hold him or her up in the air and say: "Father Sky, inspire and invigorate this young one."

5. Lay the baby down or give him or her to someone to hold while you pick up the candle and say: "Grizzly Bear, Spirit of Fire, give this young one determination and courage."

6. Now hold the smudge, saying: "Eagle, Spirit of Air, give this young one lofty ideals and imagination."

7. Now hold up the bowl of water, saying: "Coyote, Spirit of Water, give this young one love and joy."

8. Finally take a handful of salt, saying: "Buffalo, Spirit of Earth, give this young one stability and strength."
9. Each person should now come forward with a petal and place it on the baby, giving him or her a gift-wish, such as confidence or laughter.
10. Finally, smudge the crystal and dedicate it to the baby. Keep it in the baby's nursery from now on.

Lay out all the ingredients needed for the blessing before you begin.

WHEN SOMEONE DIES

WHAT DO YOU DO WHEN SOMEONE DIES? IN OUR MODERN SOCIETY WE SO OFTEN LACK MEANINGFUL RITUALS THAT HELP US COPE. THIS BLESSING IS PROFOUNDLY HEALING AND SHOULD HELP YOU SEE DEATH AS A TRANSITION, NOT AN ENDING.

Western society tends to depict death as dark, bleak, and predatory, as in this nineteenth-century painting by Evelyn Morgan. This blessing helps you to see death as transitional rather than final.

you will need

- Smudge stick
- Matches
- Bowl or shell
- Large feather
- Candle
- Sandalwood and juniper oils (optional)

INSTRUCTIONS

1. Smudge yourself to shift the outer layers of grief; smudging will also dispel any other negative emotions, such as fear or anger.

2. Sit down in a quiet place and light your candle, and if you choose, use your sandalwood and/or juniper oils. Sandalwood can help mark transitions; juniper supports the spirit in difficult times.

3. Spend some time quietly breathing and thinking about the person who has died. What were his or her good points and faults? Was there anything you left unsaid?

4. Call on your guardian angel or Spirit Animal (see pages 20–21) to accompany you down into Mother Earth. You enter via a cave in the side of a mountain and descend slowly down, down, down into the embrace of Mother Earth. Here in the darkness the bodies of all souls come to be reunited with the Mother of us all.

5. You will find yourself at the edge of a huge lake. Around you are the spirits of those who have died. You will see the person you know and approach him or her. Spend some time talking, telling him or her all your thoughts and feelings. Listen in return.

6. Turn to your guardian. You will be given a shining coin that gleams with a pure bright light. Hand it to the person you know with unconditional love. Let the person go.

7. Watch as the person gets into a beautiful boat that is waiting. He or she waves as the boat moves off, toward a blissful shining light. Retrace your steps back up through the earth.

8. Come back to waking consciousness and give thanks to Mother Earth and Father Sky for caring for the soul of the person who has died. Thank your guardian and ask him or her to care for you too, in the difficult time ahead.

In this ritual you are asked to imagine yourself entering the earth. Our ancestors also connected the earth to the afterlife and carved sacred tombs in mountainsides.

RITUAL FOR SEPARATION OR DIVORCE

THE HURT, PAIN, AND ANGER OF SEPARATION OR DIVORCE CAN BE ALMOST UNBEARABLE, BUT LIFE HAS TO GO ON. THIS RITUAL HELPS YOU CUT THE TIES AND LEAVE YOUR OLD RELATIONSHIP BEHIND YOU, ALLOWING YOU TO MOVE ON.

you will need

- Smudge stick
- Matches
- Bowl or shell
- Large feather
- Aromatherapy burner
- Lemon or lavender oils
- Walnut Bach Flower Remedy
- Glass of spring water

INSTRUCTIONS

1. Smudge yourself, asking Buffalo to help you start to release the pain and hurt. Commit yourself to the purpose of letting go.

2. Light your aromatherapy burner and add three drops of lemon and/or lavender oil. Lemon helps you accept change and let go; lavender gives resolution and helps you to release negative emotions.

The refreshing aromas of lemon and lavender are renowned for diffusing negative emotions, allowing room for change.

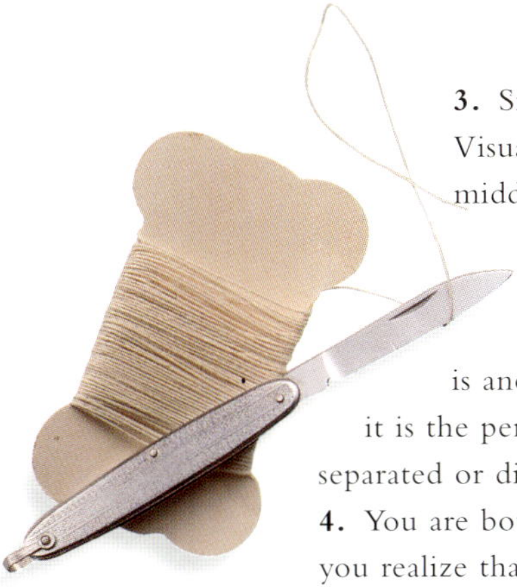

3. Sit quietly and breathe deeply. Visualize yourself standing in the middle of a magical circle. You feel totally safe and protected – nothing can hurt you within the circle's boundaries. There is another circle nearby and within it is the person from whom you have separated or divorced.

4. You are both safe within your circles but you realize that there is a shimmering thread between your solar plexus areas still joining you.

By physically cutting a tie, you can more easily acknowledge separation from a partner.

5. Take this opportunity to say anything you wish to say. Remember that you had good times as well as bad. If you possibly can, send love and forgiveness to this person – it will help to release you.

6. Now turn around. On the ground is a silver knife. Pick it up and carefully cut the cord saying: "I now release us from our past relationship with love and forgiveness."

7. You will feel a tingle of energy as the psychic tie is cut. Spend some time focusing, and imagine how you will move forward with your new life. Then come back to waking consciousness.

8. Take four drops of Walnut Bach Flower Remedy in a glass of spring water. This will help your transition to a new life. Take it whenever you need extra help and strength in the time that follows.

Water has cleansing properties. When you have completed this ritual, drink a glass of spring water with four drops of Walnut Bach Flower Remedy.

CHAPTER THREE

SEASONAL RITUALS

OUR ANCESTORS MARKED THE YEAR WITH A PRECISE PATTERN OF SEASONAL RITUALS AND CEREMONIES. THEY FOLLOWED THE RHYTHMS OF THE YEAR, CELEBRATING THE PASSING OF EACH SEASON WITH JOY AND GRATITUDE. SEASONAL RITUALS DREW FAMILIES AND COMMUNITIES TOGETHER AT REGULAR INTERVALS AND CONNECTED EVERYONE WITH THE FRUITFUL EARTH.

THE IMPORTANCE OF SEASONAL RITUALS

We are all children of the earth, and the deep rhythms of nature run through us as surely as they do through the woods and the wild creatures. The ancient festivals celebrated and revered the cycles of life: birth, maturity, death, and, above all, change. Nothing in nature stands still. The year has its own rhythm – a natural energy that rises, peaks, and slowly declines. By acknowledging this annual "tide," we can live our lives in flow with the seasons, rather than at odds with nature.

Natural cycles are reflected in our lives – we mark them with celebrations such as Harvest Suppers.

There is a time for everything: for starting new enterprises; for looking deep into the psyche; for letting go. By celebrating the festivals on the Sacred Wheel of the year, we can let our lives echo the shifts and changes in nature.

THE DECLINE OF SEASONAL CELEBRATIONS

We celebrate Christmas, Easter, and Thanksgiving; some of us will attend Harvest Suppers – but in general our seasonal celebrations have become little more than commercial experiences. Most people worry about how they will afford Christmas, rather than pondering its spiritual meaning. When we were dependent on the land in more rural, agricultural communities, seasonal celebrations held deeper significance. There is evidence of seasonal changes being celebrated in different ways across the world, regardless of religious traditions.

Christmas is an ancient festival that marks the end of the year and the coming of the new year. Evergreens are brought into the home to remind us of nature's tenacity in the winter months.

When Christianity swept the Western world, seasonal rituals were seen as pagan and there were attempts to stamp them out. Where this was not possible, the rituals were given a Christian gloss to make them acceptable. However, some, like the joyously sexual Beltane, were considered irredeemable!

RECLAIMING SEASONAL RITUALS

In this chapter, the main ideas behind the ancient seasonal rituals are reintroduced. These rituals are free of overtly religious influences and can be easily adapted to reflect your faith or philosophy. It is worth remembering too that the seasonal rituals are not all about light and laughter. In the Wheel of the year we experience the ups and downs of life. While the spring festivals celebrate the upsurge of new life and fresh hope, the fall and winter festivals tend to be more introspective. This is just as it should be: by focusing on the very essence of the seasonal ebb and flow, we can come to accept flux and change in our own lives.

THE CYCLE OF THE YEAR

THE YEARLY CYCLE FALLS NATURALLY INTO EIGHT MAJOR CELEBRATIONS. MARKING EACH ONE, IN HOWEVER SMALL A WAY, GIVES A NATURAL GENTLE RHYTHM TO THE YEAR. CHILDREN, IN PARTICULAR, LOVE THESE CELEBRATIONS BECAUSE IT CAN OFTEN SEEM A VERY LONG TIME FROM EASTER TO CHRISTMAS. THESE PAGES GIVE THE MEANINGS OF EACH CELEBRATION AND SOME IDEAS OF HOW TO CELEBRATE THEM. IN THE CHAPTER THAT FOLLOWS WE LOOK AT THE INDIVIDUAL RITUALS.

The goddess Flora (or Spring) is depicted in this Roman fresco. She is surrounded by new flowers symbolizing new growth.

HALLOWEEN: October 31. A time of purification and renewal; Halloween or Samhain honors the descent into decay and death; it is a time to remember our ancestors.

YULE/WINTER SOLSTICE: December 21. Now generally celebrated as Christmas, this is the great festival of the family. It celebrates the people who form our circle – not necessarily the people we like, but the people we need.

IMBOLC: February 2. This is the festival of hope and trust. It comes at the time of the year when everything seems dead and yet underneath the earth, life is stirring. It is about keeping hope going when there is little outside encouragement.

SPRING EQUINOX: March 21. Spring is returning and it's time to welcome new life with the festival of the old Saxon goddess, Eostre, the goddess of the Egg. This festival is all about opening up, enjoying life, and looking to the future.

BELTANE: May 1. The great fire festival, which celebrates sexuality, energy, and freedom, is also about making decisions, balancing opportunities, and is the traditional time to make a vow. However, the energy of Beltane is fresh and headstrong, and many relationships often break up around this time too.

SUMMER SOLSTICE: June 21. Summer Solstice celebrates society and our place in it. It's about learning your place in the world and healing the larger community. The festival is held outside, often ending with the rise of the sun at dawn.

LAMMAS: August 1. Lammas is the Saxon name that comes from "Loafmas" (the first loaf of the harvest), when the first grain is cut. Everyone, even vegetarians, has to kill in order to live, and at this festival we give thanks for what we have enjoyed in the past year.

FALL EQUINOX: September 21. This is a purification festival. It is time to say farewell to the warm, gentle summer and ready ourselves for the cold, harder days of winter.

As the summer ends, and the leaves on trees turn brown and gold, we are reminded of nature's cycle and the passage of time.

IMBOLC (OR CANDLEMASS) RITUAL

IMBOLC, WHICH FALLS ON FEBRUARY 2, IS THE OLD CELTIC FESTIVAL OF PURIFICATION AND HOPE. IN NATIVE AMERICAN TRADITION IT FALLS IN THE CLEANSING TIME. THIS SIMPLE CEREMONY CELEBRATES THE SMALL HOPES AND DREAMS WE ALL HAVE.

The ritual of Imbolc is celebrated on February 2, just as new growth bursts into the world.

you will need

- Lots of tiny candles or night lights
- Drum
- Smudge stick
- Matches
- Bowl or shell

INSTRUCTIONS

1. Perform this ritual after daylight has faded. Sit or lie quietly on the floor. If you are feeling stressed or tense carry out the Deep Relaxation exercise (see pages 24–25).

2. Imagine you are a seed, deep in the arms of Mother Earth. The earth is cold, dark, and hard, but you can sense that there is light above you. Imagine yourself slowly, slowly pushing upward toward the air. It is difficult, as life often is, but you know you can make it.

3. Visualize yourself breaking through the hard crust of the earth. You feel the cool air on your face. You stretch up toward Father Sky with confidence, knowing you have firm roots in Mother Earth.

4. Open your eyes and light the first small candle. Softly start to beat your drum. Imagine you are calling new life out of the earth. Think of any small hopes and dreams you have for the year – imagine you are gently coaxing them into reality.

It is traditional to light lots of small candles as part of the Imbolc or Candlemass ceremony.

5. Slowly light more candles, one by one. As the room fills with light, the sound of your drumbeat should become firmer and more insistent.

6. When all the candles are lit, stop drumming. The room is full of tiny lights; the new life under the earth is coming back. Your hopes are on their way to becoming reality.

7. End your ceremony by smudging yourself and any others to purify yourself and make way for the new. If you have animals, smudge them too.

Some people exchange small presents as part of the Imbolc celebration.

NOTE: *children love this ceremony. You may wish to include the giving of tiny presents.*

MAY DAY RITUAL

MAY DAY (MAY 1), OR BELTANE, IS ONE OF THE ANCIENT CELTIC FIRE FESTIVALS. IT CELEBRATES THE UPSURGE OF NEW LIFE, CREATIVITY, AND SEXUALITY. IN THE NATIVE AMERICAN TRADITION IT ALLIES WITH THE GROWING TIME – A PERIOD OF INTENSE ENERGY AND VITALITY.

Try to celebrate this festival in a quiet place, close to nature.

INSTRUCTIONS

1. Find a quiet place in peaceful, natural surroundings where you won't be disturbed. If it is safe to do so, light a fire and gather around it (if not, light a candle in a jar or lantern). Smudge yourself and any others present.

2. Lie down on the earth, spreading out around the fire as if you were spokes on a wheel. Note: if the ground is wet use blankets or groundsheets. Feel the earth beneath you. Breathe deeply and feel the energy and vigor of nature all around you. Ask to be filled with the wonderful feeling of joy, as well as lots of that vital energy.

3. Make garlands from wood or plant stems. Add wild flowers, as long as they are growing in profusion.

4. Start drumming, trying to mirror the rhythm of nature all around you. Dance freely around the fire. May Day is a time of testing and playful conflict so you may feel like mock fighting or wrestling. Equally it is a time of love and romance so you may want to dance with a partner.

you will need

- Candle in a jar or lantern
- Smudge stick
- Matches
- Bowl or shell
- Large feather
- Young wood or plant stems
- Wild flowers or blossoms
- Drums
- Food and drink (a May Cup is traditional)

5. When you are all exhausted, sit down around the fire and share a picnic. Pass a traditional May Cup (a fruit drink) around.

6. Remember to clear everything away and to put out the fire safely when you have finished enacting this ritual.

Fire plays an important part in other world religions. This ritual from the Bahamas involves lively colorful masks and is performed around a fire, just like the West's May Day ritual.

HOW TO MAKE A MAY CUP

(ENOUGH FOR 12 LARGE SERVINGS)

1. Warm 5 sprigs of woodruff in a very cool oven for 5 minutes.

2. Mash/crush 4 cups of strawberries with sugar to taste (approximately half a cup).

3. Stir in 4 cups of Mosel (or another crisp fragrant white wine) and 8 sprigs of fresh woodruff.

4. Leave covered in refrigerator overnight.

5. Sieve the mixture, squeeze strawberries through.

6. Decorate with a few sprigs of woodruff, small strawberries, and edible flowers if desired.

LAMMAS

THIS IS THE GREAT THANKSGIVING TIME OF THE NORTHERN HEMISPHERE (AUGUST 1). IN NATIVE AMERICAN TRADITION IT IS THE RIPENING TIME, A CHANCE TO REFLECT ON THE BOUNTY OF MOTHER EARTH AND THE RICHNESS (BOTH MATERIAL AND METAPHORICAL) IN OUR LIVES. THIS RITUAL RECONNECTS US TO THE LAND AND ITS SEASONAL CYCLE.

The bounty of nature reaches fruition at the time of Lammas, the ritual of thanksgiving. This is a time to harvest and appreciate the earth's fruits.

you will need

- Smudge stick
- Matches
- Bowl or shell
- Large feather
- A drum (optional)
- A loaf of bread or some cornmeal
- Ears of grain (optional)

INSTRUCTIONS

1. Ideally this ceremony should be performed outdoors, under the warm rays of the harvest sun. Stand quietly for a few minutes, feeling the earth underneath your feet, and your face caressed by the sunshine. If you are indoors, use your powers of visualization.

2. Smudge yourself and any others with you. Place the smudge in its bowl (but don't put it out yet).

3. If you have a drum, start to beat it with a steady, joyful, and confident rhythm. Walk or dance clockwise in a large

circle. Be very conscious of your feet on the earth and the sun on your face.

4. Come into the center of your circle, and raising your arms and face up to the sun, say: "I give thanks, great Father Sun, for the first fruits of the harvest."

5. Now lie down on the earth, spreading out your arms, and say: "I give thanks, dear Mother Earth, for the harvest of your womb."

Gather breadcrumbs and scatter them on the ground as an offering to the spirits of the harvest – earth and sun.

6. Take some cornmeal or break off crumbs of bread and scatter them on the ground as an offering to the sun, the earth, and the spirits of the harvest.

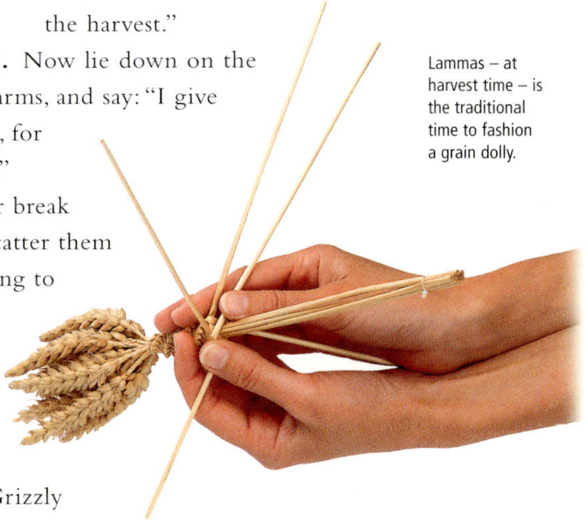

Lammas – at harvest time – is the traditional time to fashion a grain dolly.

7. Now take your smudge and offer a blessing to the four guardian spirits (Coyote, Grizzly Bear, Eagle, and Buffalo).

8. Sit quietly in a circle and think of the blessings you have, such as food, health, happiness, confidence, and loved ones. Give thanks for them all.

9. If you have access to grain, this is a lovely time to fashion a grain dolly or simply tie ears of grain together with a ribbon. Keep it in your home as a reminder of this day.

HALLOWEEN

HALLOWEEN (OCTOBER 31) IS THE ANCIENT FESTIVAL OF THE DEAD AND THE UNKNOWN. IN NATIVE AMERICAN TRADITION IT IS THE FROST TIME, A TIME TO CLEAR AWAY THE OLD AND UNNECESSARY. THIS QUIET CEREMONY PROVIDES A BALANCE TO ALL THE WILD TRICK OR TREATING!

you will need

- Candle
- Smudge stick
- Matches
- Bowl or shell
- Large feather
- Paper and pen

INSTRUCTIONS

1. Light the candle – let this be the only light in the room.

2. Smudge yourself and any others present.

3. Sit quietly and think back over the last year. What mistakes did you make? What do you regret? Write down your thoughts.

4. Now take another piece of paper and think about the year ahead. What are your fears? Now think of life in general: is there anything that scares you? Write down all your fears.

5. Now call on Grizzly Bear who can bestow courage, and Buffalo who teaches acceptance of things we can't change – he helps us let go of things we don't need. Ask these two to assist you in releasing your fears and accepting those that will not go away.

Native North Americans perform a ritual dance to celebrate the Frost Time.

Write down your feelings about the past year.

6. Feel the gentle strength and love of these spirit guardians around you. Offer some smudge to them in thanks.

7. Now carefully commit your papers to the flames. Watch them go up in smoke and imagine your fears disappearing with the burned paper.

8. It's traditional to leave your candle burning all night to guide the souls of the dead. Make sure it is safely in a bowl of water or sand and out of reach of children and animals.

HEALING DURING HALLOWEEN

Halloween is the traditional time for reading fortunes with runes, tarot cards, or the I Ching. You should also use it as a time to remember those who have passed on: get out old photograph albums; take flowers to a relative's grave; remember the old days. This is a time to visit family or friends.

Encourage children to talk about their fears of death, illness, and the unknown. Many children have fears that they don't feel they can talk about. Letting them take part in this ritual could be very healing.

The long-established practice of tarot reading is one of the many ways in which we try to predict our fates and fortunes.

CHRISTMAS/WINTER SOLSTICE

MAKE TIME AMID THE HURLY-BURLY OF THE TRADITIONAL CHRISTMAS FOR THIS SIMPLE, THOUGHTFUL RITUAL. IT CONNECTS US TO THE OLD MIDWINTER FESTIVAL OF THE DEATH AND REBIRTH OF THE SUN. IN NATIVE AMERICAN TRADITION IT FALLS AT THE BEGINNING OF THE RENEWAL TIME.

In the depth of winter we need a ritual to remind us of the sun's power and the prospect of spring.

you will need

- Paper and pen
- Candles
- Smudge stick
- Matches
- Bowl or shell
- Large feather

INSTRUCTIONS

1. Start this ritual at dusk, as the light is fading and the night is drawing in. Ideally, it should be performed with the whole family or a group of friends, but it can be done alone. If you are in a group, sit quietly in a circle.

2. Spend some time thinking about the people who are important to you. Above all, think about your family. If you are on bad terms with anyone, can you find it in your heart to forgive that person? If you are on good terms, remember that person and give thanks. If you are in a group, you may like to say your thoughts out loud.

3. Imagine you could give a gift (not a material one but some quality, such as independence) to the people in your circle and those you love. Write it on a small piece of paper and give or send it to the person in question. You may choose to read out the gifts you receive or keep them private.

4. By now it should be getting dark. Allow yourself to sit quietly in the dark for a while. As the last light fades away say: "The sun has died. The old year is passed." Pause for a few moments and then light the first candle, saying: "The sun is arisen. The new year has come." Light more candles until the room becomes quite bright.

5. Smudge yourself and everyone with you. Offer smudge in thanks for the rebirth of the sun.

Even if the ground is covered with snow and all the trees have lost their leaves, remember that spring is coming and a new year is ahead of you.

CHAPTER FOUR

PERSONAL BLESSINGS

PERSONAL BLESSINGS AND RITUALS OFFER A WAY OF RECONNECTING WITH OURSELVES DURING THE BUSTLE OF EVERYDAY LIFE. THEY GIVE US A CHANCE TO STOP AND CENTER OURSELVES, TO STEP BACK AND GAIN PERSPECTIVE ON THE WORLD AROUND US. DURING A FRENETIC DAY, PERSONAL RITUALS ALLOW US TIME FOR OURSELVES, A FEW MINUTES TO STOP AND BE QUIET, BEFORE RETURNING TO OUR BUSINESS REFRESHED AND REVITALIZED.

Rhythmic walking can offer us a form of meditation.

THE MIRACLE OF MINDFULNESS

Many personal rituals emphasize the importance of mindfulness. This is a simple technique that has been proven invaluable in the control and treatment of stress. All it involves is an awareness of where you are at that moment. Several blessings in this chapter involve elements of mindfulness but you can easily incorporate the technique into everyday life without the need for a complicated ritual. Try the following:

WALKING MEDITATION: As you walk to the bus station or to your office, try to become aware of your walking. Feel your feet firmly on the ground beneath you; feel the air on your face; and become conscious of your breathing.

Try to make meals an important part of your day – take your time to appreciate your food.

MEALTIME BLESSING: The most powerful way to bless your food is to become truly aware of it and the process of eating. Look at your meal. Take in the colors, the smell, and the arrangement of the food on the plate. Now take a mouthful and really taste the food. How does it feel? What is its texture? How exactly does it taste? Try to remain aware throughout your meal.

DRIVING AWARENESS: Most of us drive in a kind of trance. Become conscious of your driving: feel your hands on the wheel; your feet on the pedals. How are your shoulders? Tense? Imagine them relaxing. For as long as you can, be aware of what you are doing. Set up a running commentary: "There's a red car behind me; a turning coming up on the left; it's a bright day; I should check my mirror again." Not only are you practicing mindfulness; you will also be a safer driver.

Driving can provide you with an opportunity to focus on your awareness.

BLESSINGS FOR EVERY PART OF YOUR LIFE

Have fun with these rituals! Use the examples given in this chapter as a starting point for your own blessings and ceremonies. Do you hate Mondays? Why not devise a "making-Monday-happy" blessing? Are you taking part in a competition? Make up a "good luck" ceremony to bring confidence. You can have ceremonies and blessings for anything – from meeting friends to finishing work. They need not be complicated – just a few moments of visualization or meditation to mark a transition or something special.

WAKE UP AND GREET THE DAY

START EACH MORNING WITH THIS SIMPLE CLEANSING RITUAL AND YOU WILL SAIL THROUGH THE DAY FULL OF CONFIDENCE, ENERGY, AND HOPE.

How many of us wake up to the jarring noise of an alarm clock?

you will need

- Smudge stick
- Matches
- Bowl or shell
- Large feather
- Geranium essential oil plus a burner or bowl of hot water
- A candle

INSTRUCTIONS

1. Lie in bed quietly for a few moments, gently bringing yourself back to the waking world. Before getting up, tell yourself this is the start of a brand new day, full of exciting new possibilities.

2. Slowly unfold yourself and climb out of bed. Light your smudge stick or oil burner and candle. You can either smudge yourself or instead put five drops of geranium oil into the burner or bowl of hot water. Let the aroma fill the room.

3. Stand barefoot looking toward the sun or, if it's a cloudy day, where the sun would be. Feel your weight on the floor and say: "Mother Earth, keep me safe and grounded throughout this day."

4. Stretch yourself up toward the sky and say: "Father Sky, give me the confidence to fly like an eagle today."

5. Move your feet slightly wider and stretch your arms out above

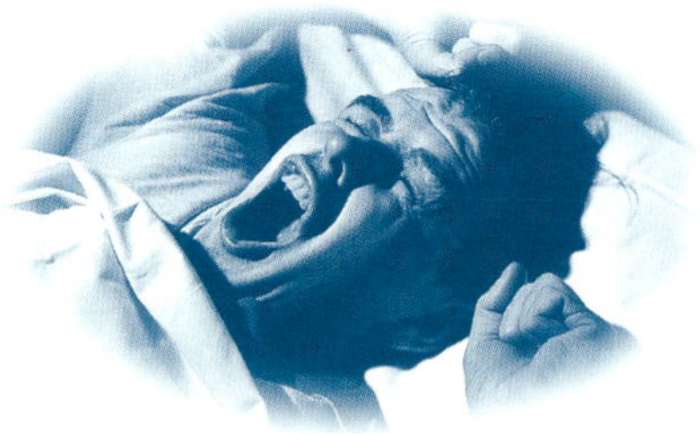

Alternatively, a few quiet moments before you wake could help to start the day more positively.

shoulder height so that you make a star-shape with your body. Say: "May the elements balance within me to give me strength, wisdom, peace, and joy this day." Visualize a warm glow in the area of your solar plexus.

6. Now sit quietly in front of your candle and think through the day ahead. Visualize yourself doing all you need to do, easily and effectively. Gently blow out your candle.

Raise your hands and give thanks for day in this early morning ritual.

SWEET DREAMS

THIS GENTLE BEDTIME CLEANSING MARKS THE CHANGE FROM DAY TO NIGHT AND EASES YOU INTO THE WORLD OF SWEET DREAMS AND DEEP, ENVIGORATING SLEEP.

you will need

- Oil burner
- Lavender oil
- Crystal

INSTRUCTIONS

1. Have a soothing bath (see Bathtime Relaxation ritual, pages 88–89). As you take off your clothes, visualize all your daytime anxieties and concerns dropping away from you. As you remove any makeup and brush your teeth, imagine any negativity felt during the day being cleansed away.

Part of preparing for bed involves washing away the day's dirt.

2. Light an oil burner and put it by the side of your bed and add four drops of lavender oil. If you prefer, you could put the oil on a kleenex and keep it by your pillow. Place your crystal by your bed to protect you through the night.

Gentle and secure sleep is a fundamental part of life.

3. Lie down, and as you breathe in the soothing scent of the oil, cast your mind back over the day. Review it without judgment. Start at the beginning and end as you are now, in bed.

4. If you are feeling tense run through the Deep Relaxation technique (see pages 24–25).

NOTE:
it is safer not to use your smudge stick for late-night cleansing because of the slight danger of sparks.

5. Is anything still worrying you? Scribble down any worrying thoughts on a pad, which you should keep by your bed just in case. You can deal with them in the morning.

6. Now ask Buffalo, guardian of dreams, to stand guard over your bed and send you sweet or useful dreams. If you have your own Spirit Animal you could ask it to accompany you on a healing or useful journey in your sleep.

7. Blow out your burner and feel the soft sweet breath of Buffalo brush gently against your cheek as you drop into a deep, peaceful sleep.

The Great Buffalo Spirit is known in Native North American myth to be the guardian of dreams.

BATHTIME RELAXATION RITUAL

A BATH AT THE END OF THE DAY IS THE PERFECT WAY TO UNWIND. TRY THIS SIMPLE SOOTHING RITUAL TO BANISH STRESS AND SET YOURSELF UP FOR A GOOD NIGHT´S SLEEP.

you will need

- Candles
- Soft music
- Lavender oil
- Burner
- Matches
- Epsom salts (optional)
- Flowers (optional)

INSTRUCTIONS

1. Prepare the bathroom so that you create a peaceful, inviting atmosphere for yourself. Light candles around your bathtub. Put on some soft relaxing music (use a battery-powered machine – not one plugged into the electricity supply). Burn lavender oil in your burner.

2. Your bath should be pleasantly warm, neither too hot nor too cool – just above body temperature. Add four drops of lavender oil; or, alternatively, 1lb./450g. of Epsom salts to your bath. (Note: medical practitioners advise against the use of Epsom salts for those with a heart condition or high or low blood pressure.)

3. Climb into your bath. If you like, add some flowers or petals now so that they float gently around you.

You might like to add flower petals to your evening bath to heighten your sense of inner peace.

4. Place a towel behind your head so that you can lean back and really relax. Now that you are fully organized, softly close your eyes and imagine that you are lying in a magical pool, perhaps deep in the woods, on a gorgeous beach, or even in a beautiful temple.

5. The water of this pool is healing. It draws out of you all the stresses and strains of the day – all negativity and doubts simply vaporize into the air and disappear.

6. Once you have been cleansed of all negativity, the water of the pool starts to glow with a soft, golden gleam. You begin to sense the loving presence of the Spirit of Water who wants to approach you and give you a gift. Accept it with thanks. Golden light streams into every pore of your body, bringing relaxation, joy, and peace.

7. Lie and enjoy the feeling of total relaxation. When you are ready, bid farewell to the Spirit of Water and feel your magical pool turn once again into your bathroom.

Water has long been thought to carry healing properties, and many religions perform ceremonies around pools, lakes, and oceans.

BANISHING STRESS RITUAL

WHENEVER LIFE STARTS TO GET ON TOP OF YOU, TAKE TEN MINUTES TO STOP WHAT YOU ARE DOING AND PRACTICE THIS SIMPLE, HIGHLY EFFECTIVE RITUAL. THERE ARE TWO VERSIONS – ONE FOR WHEN YOU ARE ON YOUR OWN AT HOME, AND ONE FOR WHEN YOU ARE AT WORK OR AMONG OTHER PEOPLE.

you will need

- Smudge stick
- Matches
- Bowl or shell
- Large feather
- Lavender oil
- Paper and pen

Work can often be the source of all kinds of stress and anxiety.

INSTRUCTIONS

1. If you are alone, smudge yourself. If you cannot do this, put four drops of lavender oil on a kleenex and breathe in the relaxing scent.

2. Take a few moments to write down everything that is making you feel stressed.

3. Now lie or sit down and start to notice the scent of the oil or smudge. Start to breathe more deeply and slowly – really pay attention to the scent. Ask the spirits of the smudge or lavender for their help and advice.

4. Run through the Deep Relaxation ritual (see pages 24–25). If you are at work you can do this quietly, sitting at your desk, without feeling that you are disturbing anyone else.

5. When you have finished, take yourself to a standing position (if at work, stay seated). Feel your feet firmly on the ground. Imagine them rooted solidly in the earth and ask Mother Earth to keep you grounded, with a strong sense of balance. Now imagine your head being gently pulled up toward the sky, straightening your spine and loosening your shoulders. Ask Father Sky to give you inspiration. Call on Coyote to help you to find clever solutions to your problems.

6. Look back at your list of problems and see if you have any solutions, wild ideas, thoughts, or inspiration. No need to panic if you don't – good ideas often come later.

It is possible to practice relaxation at work. Remain seated and raise your head to the sky. Keep your feet carefully rooted on the earth and ask the spirits to give you inspiration.

LOOKING FOR LOVE RITUAL

ARE YOU TRYING TO FIND A PARTNER? WOULD YOU LIKE TO INJECT SOME MORE LOVE AND PASSION INTO AN EXISTING RELATIONSHIP? TRY THIS RITUAL – IT CAN HAVE MAGICAL RESULTS!

If you are hoping to inject a bit of passion into a stale relationship, or plan to shoot Cupid's arrow at a new partner, this ritual is bound to help!

INSTRUCTIONS

1. Play some music that puts you in a romantic mood. If you have a partner, it could be "your" song that reminds you of all the good times you have spent together. If you don't have a partner, avoid music that you associate with ex-lovers.

2. Smudge yourself, asking clever Coyote to help you in your quest.

3. Think about what you want from your ideal partner. Write down all the characteristics on the piece of paper. Be precise, but avoid thinking about and asking for a particular person by name. Now write down all the reasons why you are ready at this moment for a good relationship. Finally, put down anything that might be standing in your way.

you will need

- Favorite music (optional)
- Smudge stick
- Matches
- Bowl or shell
- Large feather
- Paper and pen
- Three candles: deep red, orange, and pink
- Sharp implement such as a needle or art knife
- Ylang-ylang oil and a burner

Candlelight brings a certain magic to intimate moments.

Different-colored candles can bring different kinds of excitement to your love life.

4. On the red candle, write (using your needle or knife): "I, (your name), am now ready for passion." On the orange candle, write: "I, (your name), now choose friendship and fun." On the pink candle, write: "I, (your name), invite love and romance into my life."

5. Light your candles one by one. Light the oil burner and add two drops of ylang-ylang oil.

6. Meditate on the candle flames. Create a mental image of your prospective partner, then call out, appealing to his or her senses.

7. Carefully commit your piece of paper to the flames, asking the healing power of fire to cleanse you and clear you of anything standing in the way of love.

8. End by thanking Coyote and the spirits of the flame. If it's safe to do so, allow your candles to burn out naturally. This allows the ritual to work more deeply.

PSYCHIC PROTECTION CLEANSING

WE ALL HAVE TIMES WHEN WE FEEL UNEASY, JITTERY, OR JUST PLAIN SCARED. THIS CLEANSING RITUAL CAN HELP YOU FEEL MORE CENTERED AND PROTECTED IN THE WORLD AT LARGE.

you will need

- Smudge stick
- Bowl or shell
- Matches
- Large feather
- Crystal

INSTRUCTIONS

1. Smudge yourself and the room around you. Smudge your crystal too.

2. Place your crystal close by you to absorb any negative energy in order to gather all the strength that you need. If you are performing this cleansing before you sleep, keep your crystal by your bed.

3. Center yourself, breathe deeply and evenly.

4. Now call on the four Great Animal Spirits to cleanse and protect your space. Say: "Great Eagle, spread your wings before me. Keep me safe."

5. Next say: "Great Bear, please stand behind me. May your sharp claws protect my back."

6. Now call on Coyote saying: "Great Coyote, stand on my right and may your sharp wits protect me."

Spirit animals, such as Eagle, feature in Native American Totem poles.

7. Finally summon Buffalo: "Great Buffalo, please stand to my left and keep me and this place safe."

8. Imagine all four Great Spirits surrounding and protecting your space.

9. Carry out the Aura Cleansing ritual (see pages 26–27) and spread the bright white light to encompass the spirits and your whole room.

10. Thank the spirits and ask them to keep up their protection as long as is necessary.

INDEX